Mental health ... that few have attempted to address. ... issues on the rise and their health and wellness on the decline, Dr. Eric Block's book attempts to reverse this course. I would highly recommend you pick up a copy and learn from his wisdom.

–Christopher Phelps, DMD, CMCT

Dr. Eric Block has provided the ultimate guide for the dentist operating in a highly stressful world to embrace the thought process to become a stress-free dentist. This book should be required reading for all graduating dental students and residents.

–Jason E. Portnof DMD, MD, FACS, FICD, FACD

As dentists, it's really important that we address the topics that Dr. Eric Block discussed in The Stress-Free Dentist. With burnout among healthcare professionals at an all-time high, knowing that we have options helps us create better lives for ourselves and better care for patients.

–Dr. Laura Brenner

Dentistry is a wonderful profession but also one filled with stress and anxiety. In this book, Dr. Block shares his own story as well as others on how you can have a stress-free, abundant career and life as a dentist!

–Dr. Kimberly Nguyen

I thought this was a great book for any one in any industry. Seeing Dr. Block's concepts and real-world application was very insightful!

–Austin Hair

As someone who has been involved with his fair share of stress related issues within the dental community, mental health and wellness are two incredibly important topics that need to be addressed. Eric Block does a great job dealing with the issues that a dentist deals with while being the CEO of his office. If you want to learn how to become a stress-free dentist this is the book for you.

–Leonard F. Tau DMD,
Owner Pennsylvania Center for Dental Excellence,
Author, Raving Patients

Dentistry is a lifelong career after many years of studying and training. Dr. Block's book is of paramount importance to all graduate school and practicing dentists for the purpose of have a long and gratifying career. Only the mentally tough and resilient will make it and this book serves as the ultimate tool for career success.

–Dr. Alden Cass,
Clinical Psychologist, Performance Coach,
Competitive Streak Consulting

Avoiding burnout, stress, and overcommitment at work is more important than ever. Dr. Block provides an invaluable guide for navigating the inevitable stresses of dental practice in this new book.

–Bruce Tulgan
Author of *The Art of Being Indispensable at Work*; *Win Influence, Beat Overcommitment, and Get the Right Things Done*
(Harvard Business Review Press, 2020)

I believe this book will help many people in our profession.

–Dr. Dan B., DDS, CAGS

THE STRESS-FREE DENTIST

Overcome burnout and
start loving dentistry again

DR. ERIC BLOCK

Copyright © 2021 by Dr. Eric Block

All rights reserved. No part of this publication may be reproduced, stored in a retrieval system, or transmitted, in any form or by any means, except as may be expressly permitted by the 1976 Copyright Act or by Dr. Eric Block in writing.

ISBN: 978-1-7366589-2-5

Whilst every effort has been made to ensure that the information contained within this book is correct at the time of going to press, the author and publisher can take no responsibility for the errors or omissions contained within.

DEDICATION

This book is dedicated to all of the dental professionals out there suffering from burnout and anxiety. Trust me, you can beat this!

And, to my wife Sooann, daughter Charlotte, son Axel, mother Judy, father Dr. Michael Block, and sisters Jennifer Block Martin, and Dr. Elizabeth Block.

CONTENTS

Foreword		ix
Acknowledgments		xi
Introduction		xiii
Chapter 1	Are You Burned Out?	1
Chapter 2	Depression, Anxiety, Addiction and Pain	17
Chapter 3	People-Pleasing and Conflict Resolution	53
Chapter 4	Are You A Real Imposter?	67
Chapter 5	How to Handle Rejection and Connect With Patients	95
Chapter 6	Office Culture — Is Yours Toxic?	111
Chapter 7	Don't Let the Money Burn You	125
Chapter 8	Business Management with Boundaries	149
Chapter 9	I Beat Burnout — And You Can, Too	175
References		211

FOREWORD

Dr. Block and I run in similar circles, but didn't connect until COVID hit. With most dentists out of work for a bit, Dr. Block didn't just sit on his hands and wait it out—he took the opportunity of time out of the office to build something new: Deals for Dentists.

As someone who deeply respects those who are able to overcome the barriers put in front of them, I was 100% on board with Dr. Block's project. His COVID-born-side-hustle included a great podcast and Dr. Block and I had an amazing time discussing some of the issues important to dentists. As we talked, I learned more and more about Dr. Block's own story as a dentist. Specifically, how he went through a really hard period and nearly left the profession. It struck me that one of the most stressful things I can think of, after 22 years in the profession, is running a dental practice.

Practice owners are expected to be CEO, HR, Payroll, Marketing Strategists, and Psychologists…as well as practitioners. The overwhelming amount of pressure of leading a team while also making patients happy is enough to push anyone over the edge. As someone who acquired a dental office after the suicide of the previous owner, I know first-hand the devastation that can occur in our profession.

Dr. Block will tell you that he was nearly buried by his work, but was able to recognize something was wrong, and go get help.

His book is not only the story of how he overcame burnout by building systems to support his mental health, but is also relatable and chock-full of actionable things any dentist can do to help themselves support their mental wellbeing and build a practice they love.

Even before COVID-19 dentists were stressed, and now things are even worse. Now is the perfect time for over-worked, over-stressed dentists, dental students, and dental teams to take a hard look at their coping strategies. This book is a must-read for anyone feeling the burn of burnout. You will learn ways to hold healthy boundaries, find joy in your work, and go home at the end of the day excited to go back to work tomorrow.

Dr. Block hit it out of the park with this one. I'm confident it can help anyone as much, or more, than it's helped me.

Leonard F. Tau

OWNER, PENNSYLVANIA CENTER FOR DENTAL EXCELLENCE
GM, DENTAL BIRDEYE

ACKNOWLEDGMENTS

I would like to thank everyone whose work has inspired and challenged me. Also a huge thank you to those who encouraged me to write this book. I couldn't have done it without your support.

Dr. Howard Farran	Dr. Len Tau
Elijah Desmond, RDH	Dr. Alden Cass
Dr. Laura Brenner	Dr. Dan B.
Dino Watt	Jason E. Portnof DMD, MD, FACS, FICD, FACD
Dr. Kimberly Nguyen	
Dr. Al Hawryluk	Jeremy SantaCroce, RN/NP, LICSW
Dr. Alireza Moheb	Phil Herndon MA, LPC-MHSP, NCC
Dr. Cory Glenn	
Austin Hair	Dr. Joshua Puckett
Author Bruce Tulgan	Dr. Chris Phelps, CMCT
Dr Paul Etchison	Dr. Sonia Hariri

INTRODUCTION

I dreaded going to work. The profession was suffocating me. When I left for the day and went home, I felt like I could finally breathe. I was angry at myself for choosing the profession of dentistry.

I was up all night, tossing and turning with the days' stresses playing on a loop in my mind. I knew I needed help, but I didn't want to bother the seasoned staff or the front desk to help me. I was getting an ulcer from the stress of avoiding conflict. I spent a long time as an associate, trying to live by the owner's rules and making sure that patients were happy with my work.

I had started out excited to help patients, but as I struggled to connect with them, I started worrying every day—what if a procedure that wasn't 100% perfect and made a patient mad, and they sued me?

Dental school was already hard enough. Good grades didn't come easily to me, and I had to work hard to get my degree. But then things only got tougher. School didn't teach me anything about business management. I didn't have training on how to deal with the emotional side of the profession—how to deal with staff, how to talk to patients, how to see and manage my own stress. I learned how to treat patients, but I didn't know how to treat myself.

My way of trying to solve my problems was to try to get tougher on myself. I said "no" to myself—no to rest and to boundaries—so that I could say "yes" to everyone else. I sacrificed my own health and happiness to try to avoid every confrontation.

Like many other dentists, I'm an introvert, and this added another dimension to my struggle. I was going from room to room, trying to keep on a happy face while treating patients the best I could, feeling the pressure to look like I was totally happy and totally in control. After all, I needed to manage my patient's anxiety—but the irony was, I couldn't manage my own.

I looked at the prospect of doing this for another thirty years and began to regret my choice of career. I was tired of being nervous all the time and afraid of being sued. I imagined how nice it would be to be a landscaper or to sit in a cubicle and not have to talk to anyone. Maybe I could go to law school and become a lawyer so I could be the one to do the suing. But I'd already gotten hundreds of thousands of dollars into debt just to finish dental school and didn't have the mental energy to go back to school or go deeper into debt.

I was stuck and I needed to make my job work, but I wasn't sure how. The solutions I kept trying to apply—pleasing people, trying harder, constantly worrying—not only weren't solving my real problems, but they were also adding a whole new set of their own. My emotional and physical exhaustion built to the point where I finally said, "This is no way to live."

I Was One Stressed-Out Dentist

When people are feeling burnt out or really stressed by their job, that seeps into all parts of their lives. Was I a bad dentist? No. A bad person? Absolutely not. I was doing the best I could with the tools I had, but my mental tools weren't good nough.

INTRODUCTION

We spend a lot of our life at work, and being miserable for several hours a day takes a toll. As you probably know, this kind of stress affects every aspect of our lives—not just the professional, but also the personal.

It's like we start to disappear. There isn't enough of us to go around. There's less of us for our families, for our hobbies. We start withdrawing and isolating. Some of us experience emotional and physical pain, and our suffering may drive us to depend on pain medication, or possibly we self-medicate through alcohol or other substances.

Some of us will struggle so much with our career that, even after massive investments of time and money, we walk away. Some of us just wish we could. We keep going through the motions, showing up at a job that may increasingly feel like it's asking everything of us while giving little back. And because of the nature of our training and our profession, many of us don't have the tools we need to prevent or treat burnout.

That's the bad news.

But here's the good news: There's hope.

Recovery from burnout is possible. Many people have found a way to address the stress and rediscover the joy in their professional and personal lives. You'll need to take time and make changes, but you can find a way to make your job work for you. And when you solve the stresses that contribute to professional burnout, your personal life will benefit, too.

Now, by no means do I consider myself an authority figure. I'm a dentist, like you. I'm someone who's been there, who *was* burnt out, but who's found his way back. I'm someone who's sat where you sit and who knows firsthand the anxiety that so many dentists struggle with. I've had ups and downs, I've made mistakes and learned from them, and I've connected with some amazing people who have stories and solutions of their own to share.

Burnout? I've been there. But I've come back from it, and I want to help you do the same. Or better yet, completely avoid it.

How to Use This Book

I've structured this book like a mini-workshop. I know we're busy professionals, and chances are, if you're reading this, you're already dealing with the stress that affects so many of us. Stress affects our ability to focus and retain, and many of us are likely juggling the complications burnout can bring to both our professional and personal lives.

With that in mind, I've kept each solution-focused. They're like classes where we'll go over common issues like People-Pleasing, Anxiety, Perfectionism, and Imposter Syndrome.

With each chapter, we'll assess how we've been affected by these common struggles. I'll give you the tools you need to assess yourself, I'll let you know it's not just you, and then I'll give you key takeaways and game-changing solutions that have made my dental career more enjoyable and less stressful.

Added to each chapter are quotes from interviews I've done with mental health professionals, life coaches, and fellow dentists. These wonderful people candidly share their experiences with things like shame, sexual harassment, addiction, and also turning points, breakthroughs, and recovery.

It was vital to me to include these in this book because burnout's buddies are isolation and withdrawal, and one of the best ways to block that is with peer engagement. Peer engagement is crucial for many reasons.

First, because a burden shared is a burden lessened. Stress is hard enough without struggling alone and ashamed, and knowing you're not alone can lift that burden of shame and, hopefully, give you enough oomph to make the changes that could take your life back to a better place.

Second, because the stories of others hold up a mirror to ourselves. Sometimes it's hard to see how symptoms of stress manifest in our lives, especially if we've gotten locked into patterns like perfectionism. It can be easier to recognize our own patterns and struggles when we hear others share theirs.

We're dentists, and we know that good treatments require accurate assessment. The solutions we need depend upon seeing ourselves and our struggles clearly, and having the support of others' stories near us can give us the support we need to stand the pain of opening our eyes.

So, whether you want to jump to chapters that apply most clearly to you or just start here at the beginning and read straight through, my hope is that you'll make my book work for you, according to the time and energy you have. Those of you in deep burnout, who are exhausted and struggling with focus and time, may want to skim the final chapter, where I'll include bullet points from the entire book.

But I do hope you'll at least dip your toe in chapters that you think don't apply because you may be surprised. I sure was when my therapist told me I had anxiety! And, even if something doesn't apply to you yet—younger dentists, grads, I'm looking at you—make yourself familiar with the common contributing factors of burnout so that you can put together a plan of preventive care that will ensure you see and solve stress before it burns you out.

The most important thing is that you pick something to learn about and find some kind of action to take. This problem isn't going away on its own. But, thankfully, you're not on your own trying to fight it. There are great mentors, coaches, and therapists out there who want to help you.

The single most rewarding thing about my work with helping dentists is when a dentist comes in to talk to me. They're at the end of their rope—burned out, anxious, depressed, hating the profession. I witness their first tears as they're processing their story for the first time. And then, I'm watching that limbic revision take place.

A lament comes out of these very high octane people, who have so much brain power. They are so tough and want to do well, and they come into my office where they don't have to do any of that anymore. They can just be themselves. When that happens, out comes the grief and the sadness and anger and loneliness or whatever else they had put aside, maybe since first grade, to get those academics done and to succeed and be spit out on the other end.

One of my greatest joys is working with these very high-octane, intelligent people because they can take that massive intellect and ability to get things done and then go do what they're made to do and serve society where they're really needed.

–PHIL HERNDON MA, LPC-MHSP, NCC

Dentistry is a physically and mentally demanding profession. If you don't take care of your mental health, it will beat you down and burn you out. The sooner you can block burnout, the sooner you can get back to looking forward to going to work everything. You deserve nothing less.

We'll do this together. Let's find a way to make your job work for you.

CHAPTER 1
ARE YOU BURNED OUT?

Have you found yourself thinking any of these things?
"I'm always nervous when I think about my day."
"I don't know if that clinical work I did yesterday was good enough."
"What if I get a bad review? What would the owner think?"
"I'm afraid of going to work."
"Does the owner like me?"
"I'm afraid of dealing with the front desk."
"Oh, no, what if that patient doesn't like me?"
"What if a patient sues me?"
"Am I going to lose my job?"
"I need this job! ... But I don't want to go to work."
If you answered yes, then you might be suffering from burnout.

What is Work-Related Burnout?

Some people think "burnout" is just another term for feeling stress, usually at work. Chronic stress is not your staff standing outside your office waiting to ask you the same question someone else just asked you, the pile of bills you stuff in a portfolio for the bookkeeper to handle, or the difficult patients you would rather dismiss than treat. Though those things do cause stress, they don't lead to burnout unless the stress is never addressed.

[1]Chronic stress is an internal, biological, physiological, chemical reaction that is part of your autonomic nervous system, and it has clear and identifiable symptoms. And when you don't treat or manage chronic stress, burnout is the result.

Here's what burnout looks and feels like:

Physical symptoms: You might be experiencing headaches, stomachaches, GI issues, chest pain, dizziness, migraines, shortness of breath, or recurring tightness in your back, neck, and shoulders. Maybe you keep getting sick, and you've lost your appetite. You should definitely try to rule out other health concerns, but also keep in mind that stress can cause (or exacerbate) all of these.

Emotional exhaustion: Fatigue that doesn't seem to go away even with sleep—if you *can* sleep. Insomnia, feelings of guilt, lack of interest in things you used to enjoy. You may be feeling drained, unable to cope, and struggling to complete work tasks. Maybe you're even feeling constant worry and dread about work and life.

Reduced work performance: Everyday tasks at work that used to be doable feel increasingly impossible, and your work is piling up. You have difficulty focusing on tasks and are increasingly rigid about how to complete them. Your creativity and tolerance levels are bottoming out. You keep showing up late, you're missing meetings, you forget important details, and you start avoiding work in order to manage this drop in performance.

Alienation from work: You see your job as stressful and

---

[1] **How Real Dentists Conquer Real Stress**
In-text: (How real dentists conquer real stress, 2021)
Your Bibliography: DentistryIQ. 2021. *How real dentists conquer real stress.* [online] Available at: <https://www.dentistryiq.com/practice-management/practice-management-tips/article/16367701/how-real-dentists-conquer-real-stress> [Accessed 28 February 2021].

frustrating, and you're growing cynical about your workplace and the people you're around. You have less and less tolerance for things that feel wrong, inefficient, or stupid, and you find yourself resenting people. You're increasingly isolated and keep finding ways to get out of meetings or talking to others, especially coworkers. You're feeling distant and numb.

These things—pain and exhaustion, cynicism, and feelings of reduced professional ability—are the hallmarks of burnout. Together, these symptoms lead to an inability to function on a personal and professional level successfully.

Many symptoms of anxiety and depression overlap with burnout. We'll go into more depth in a later chapter about how anxiety and depression interact with burnout and how their treatments complement each other. You may have also noticed that the signs and symptoms of burnout overlap with stress. That's because stress + time = burnout.

Ignoring the warning signs of chronic stress leads to headaches, forgetfulness, fatigue, mood swings, sleepless nights, indifference, depression, burnout, and more. Consistently, when dental professionals share how they feel, it's as if they're reciting from a medical journal about the consequences of stress. But they can't change what they don't acknowledge.

Stress prevention and management are key to blocking burnout, and the first step to managing stress is seeing it. The sooner you see the signs, the better you can block burnout. Focus on seeing the signs so you can take care of your mental health.

What I've observed is that when people are feeling burnt out or really stressed by their job, that it really seeps into all parts of their lives.

> *That includes primary relationships: family, kids, hobbies. All of that gets impacted. People isolate themselves from friends, and obviously, I'm talking pre-COVID here, but they won't*

hang out with their friends. They'll stop going to softball league; they'll find it more difficult to get out of the house because all they want to do is come home from work and just be at home.

I certainly see the impact of substance use, where people might use alcohol or other drugs to deal with the stress. That, obviously, leads people down paths that can be destructive.

And I've also seen people either walk away from careers, ones they're committed to, that they've spent their whole lives getting into or coming close to. That's really sad to see, especially if this was your passion, if it was something someone really wanted to do, and people say, I can't deal with this anymore, and just walk away. To watch people walk away from that is pretty tough to see.

So, yes. The impact of stress at work reaches into just about every facet of people's lives.

—JEREMY SANTACROCE, RN/NP, LICSW

Who Gets Burnout?

Anyone who lets their stress go unchecked can burn out, but some people are especially vulnerable.

You are at higher risk for burnout if:

- You have a high workload, including high volume and/or overtime work
- Your job is your identity, and you have a poor work/life balance
- You have to wear many hats at work, including hats for which you were never trained.
- You have little or no control over your work or environment

- Your job is monotonous
- You tend toward perfectionism and pessimism
- Your job leads to physical pain and fatigue
- You work in a helping profession, like health care

Did you, too, notice that these risk factors just described dentistry to a T?

Dentistry is many good things, but it's also a profession that's combined many risk factors for serious stress in one heavy, painful package. We're especially vulnerable to the stresses that tend to build up into burnout.

Additionally, dentists as a group tend to underreport symptoms, continue working in adverse conditions, and are more reluctant to admit to problems or to ask for help.

> *I did the first clinical investigation on the mental health of Wall Street stockbrokers in 1999, and the results that came out were highly publicized. That launched me into the Wall Street psychology world and helped me focus on a target population that was underserved and under-noticed, in terms of the clinical issues that are very common for other professions as well, including dentists, doctors, and lawyers—other professionals who are dealing with huge amounts of responsibility and high levels of stress.*
>
> *You have to become extremely depersonalized in these professions so that you don't experience the emotions—anxiety, fear of failure, need for perfection. These feelings left unchecked can damage someone's mental health and overall performance.*
>
> *Part of what I do is get under the hood with these individuals and help them by not only identifying what they're feeling in the moment but also to help manage it so*

that it's done and felt in a way that doesn't affect their overall performance.

–DR. ALDEN CASS

Do I Have Burnout?

Something I've learned about anxiety is that it's very good at justifying its existence. When you see a dentist get sued, it seems reasonable to fear that you might get sued, too. But worrying about it every day to the point that you avoid procedures or dread going to work is a sign that the stress is doing you harm.

The more anxious I was, the less I was able to see my own anxiety until my therapist pointed it out.

Many people only realized their burnout in retrospect. These stress factors combine and accumulate, and many of them seem unfixable, so we live with circumstances that aren't tolerable in the long term. Burnout tends to creep up on us, and we don't realize what a serious problem we have until it feels too late.

So, in case you're still unsure if the distress you're feeling is burnout, here's another idea for how you can determine where you are on the spectrum between stress and burnout:

The Burn Test

Try taking a vacation.

First of all, if you don't feel you can take any time off ever, that's a great indication that your work/life balance is awry and likely to lead to increasing amounts of stress. Many dentists who struggle with burnout report a common pattern of work/life imbalance. The truth is, you can choose to take time off now, or your health and sanity will force you to take time off later, in a much more painful way.

But try taking some time away from work. If your home life is stressful, maybe get a break from that as well, if you can.

If you find yourself feeling much better with that time off and your head-clearing, it's a good indication that your work life is impairing your full function as a healthy human being. That might indicate that you need to take a look at how your work life is structured.

Maybe addressing your work environment will help—are there interpersonal issues going on? Maybe you need a more ergonomic setup, or clearer communication, or better boundaries.

Going to work isn't supposed to be the same as going to Disneyland, but it's entirely reasonable and desirable that your work-life be good enough that you don't need to escape from it. You live a good part of your life at work, and you deserve to have a job you don't have to run away from.

But if even after a week or two of total relaxation, sleep, and good nutrition, you still can't seem to recover your sense of self, and you're still dreading going back to work, then you know something is seriously wrong, and it's time to figure out what that is. Don't let your job undermine your health.

> *Dentists are so good at going tooth to tooth, being systematic, doing linear problem solving using cause and effect, looking at a whole face spatial structure, how all the systems work together, and engaging from that highly scientific view of things.*
>
> *Also, almost every dentist I know is at least leaning towards introversion. I'm married to an accountant, so I've known introversion for thirty-one years. She needs time when she comes home at the end of the day, and she doesn't do tax work with a lot of people—more the ledger-bookkeeper type*

of accounting. So she doesn't have people around, but just having people around drains her.

So, part of the burnout can be being a really good scientist or technician who's needing to expend more energy socially than they would, and the compartmentalization you must do to keep doing that. The cumulative effect of that is a huge capacity to box things off, which creates a lack of internal insight— "I don't know how I got burned out; I just know I can barely get out of bed." Well, that's how you did it.

—PHIL HERNDON MA, LPC-MHSP, NCC

Yes, I'm Exhausted. What Now?

If you're burnt out, welcome to the club. You're in very good company!

Because burnout can lead us to feel alienated from our jobs and then our lives, there's something I want to get really clear: you wouldn't be hurting if you didn't care.

We got here by being hard-working students and people whose careers are dedicated to helping people. Dental school isn't easy. Moving into the real world of everyday practice is even less easy. All of us are here because we care about succeeding and striving for a higher purpose in life.

We succeeded in school, but our clinical training didn't include training in things that can come to define or even dominate our professional lives: connecting with patients, dealing with staff, managing business, and making money.

Most of us also didn't learn how to assess and treat our own mental health issues. For many of us, our health takes the backseat as we put work first. As a result, we have a major mental health problem in dentistry.

Additionally, most of us graduated with a massive amount of

student loan debt, and we have immense financial pressure to make our job work, no matter how difficult. The apathy and alienation that characterizes advanced burnout is our brain and body trying to protect us from something that they view as a threat: our job.

And they're not totally wrong. Dentistry is a physically and mentally demanding profession, and if you don't take care of yourself, your work will beat you down and burn you out.

But we're going to work together to defang this problem and make the changes and find the solutions that will make our jobs—and lives—safer and more fulfilling.

Now let's examine each of the stress factors that can turn into burnout.

> *Sometimes people approach mental health treatment as a quick fix. Like, "I just need to get back to be functional," which is certainly okay because if you're really struggling with burnout and feel like walking away from your job, it's totally appropriate that the first goal should be, let's get you there. But there's often a lot of other work to do.*
>
> *Sometimes, people don't have the time, energy, or desire to do the psychological work. Medications can only go so far. That's tough, and this year, in particular, has created so many layers of stress for people, including stress from the idea that now they have to add an hour of therapy a week, and they don't feel like they have time for that.*
>
> –JEREMY SANTACROCE, RN/NP, LICSW

Risk Factors for Burnout

High workload. Many of us go half a million dollars into debt from day one, and then we're launched into a profession where we're told to manage staff, see patients, and run a business. We have our hand in all the pots: keeping up with accounting, marketing, human resources, and managing insurance. Dentistry is frequently intense and can be overwhelming

Money and debt. We come out of school burdened with a debt equal to a mortgage but without the house. Those of us who consider transitioning to ownership of a practice face even greater financial risks. This high-stakes financial situation is even more difficult when you add in an actual house, a family, and then throw in a global pandemic.

High identification with one's job. We identify with our jobs. We feel responsible for others, especially as owners. We're the paycheck for many families and need to help people resolve issues with their teeth that cause them pain. All of this raises the emotional stake we have in our work.

Poor boundaries. In our attempt to catch up and make things work, we may engage in people-pleasing and make others a priority even to our own detriment. When we do this, our work/life balance disappears, and we become imbalanced—and exhausted.

Introversion vs. Extroversion. Introverts can be utterly exhausted by the need to be "on" for patients and staff all day, no matter how they're feeling inside, and being drained day after day takes its toll. Meanwhile, extroverts may feel limited by the roles in their office; doing the same procedures day after day can feel cumbersome for those who need a lot of stimulation to thrive.

Patient connection. Ideally, we get to be the good guys—patients come to us in pain, and we diagnose the problem and fix it. Unfortunately, a lot of people are afraid of dentists, or see us as a source of pain, and it's stressful to feel like the person most people dread to see. Additionally, all our clinical work, no matter how expert, ends up being rated by patients, so part of our job is to juggle patient expectations and management continually. That's a recipe for a lot of emotional overwork.

Isolation. Many of us are working in little bubbles, especially those of us in solo practices. After all the camaraderie of dental school, suddenly, we're faced with increasing challenges and a lack of peer engagement and support. This isolation often correlates to poor health outcomes.

Lack of professional support. Many of us launch into work and find that we suddenly need to do more clinical work with far less mentoring support than we've been accustomed to. Feeling like we're always struggling to keep up is isolating and can contribute to Imposter Syndrome, one term for how personal anxiety and poorly calibrated professional expectations can lead us to become isolated and shy away from opportunities that might help us grow.

Lack of control. An inability to influence decisions that affect your job—such as your schedule, systems, or workload—could lead to job burnout. So could a lack of the resources you need to do your work.

Unclear job expectations. If you're unclear about the degree of authority you have or what your supervisor or others expect from you, you're not likely to feel comfortable at work. Associates especially have this issue when dealing with staff—there's often a question of "who's in charge?"

Dysfunctional workplace dynamics. Perhaps you work with an office bully, or you feel undermined by colleagues, or your boss micromanages your work. Nobody thrives when they're unsupported, especially in something as important as their work.

Extremes of activity. When a job is monotonous or chaotic, you need constant energy to remain focused—which can lead to fatigue and job burnout. Additionally, holding still for long periods of time as we do chairside dentistry can lead to injuries and chronic pain.

Work-life imbalance. If your work takes up so much of your time and effort that you don't have the energy to spend time with your family and friends, you might burn out quickly. Healthy people are whole people. We need something other than work in our lives. If you're withdrawing from things you enjoy, then that's a major sign that your life is awry.

Pessimism. Dentistry is full of challenges. If we believe that our current difficulties reliably predict future and forever difficulty, it can be hard to have the hope we need and the will to make the changes we need. We also often have a false belief that dentistry is just a stressful profession, and nothing can be done about it. We tell ourselves, "That's why we get paid the big bucks." When really, it doesn't have to be this way.

Perfectionism. It's a personality type, and our expectations for ourselves are high. However, in many cases, we're not congratulated for a good job but are penalized for a bad one. This leads to constant stress and saps our feeling of pride in our work.

Stressful personal life. Those of us who are already struggling with or are at risk for anxiety, depression, and addiction are especially vulnerable to the cumulative effects of stress.

Chronic pain. Chairside clinical dentistry can lead to real issues like shoulder, neck, and back pain, and chronic pain is draining. It's absolutely reasonable not to want to keep doing something that hurts us on a regular basis.

I hope it's helpful to read these symptoms, but it's also understandable if it's discouraging. These symptoms describe a lot of what I experienced, too. It made me hate going to work for a long time. It's hard to acknowledge problems when we believe there are no solutions, and, for a long time, I didn't have solutions.

The good news is, there's hope! You've already taken the first step by picking up this book!

Do I find that some people end up leaving their profession? Where they decided it just wasn't for them; the stress was too high; it was better for them to move on and find something else to do?

We've seen that happen more with lawyers than any other profession. But I feel like that's because they can go out and do other things that relate to having a law background. I haven't seen many in the dental or optometry or plastic surgery fields shift gears like that.

I think that's partially due to how much money and time you've invested in your careers, and to just give it up would be really hard. So instead, you have to find ways to grind through and think about your job on a daily basis with a healthier mindset, one that's more adaptive.

–DR. ALDEN CASS

Should I Just Quit?

Dentistry is inherently a stressful place, and if we don't take action to notice where we're hurting, alleviate it, and change the circumstances that injure us, then we are certainly going to burn out. Some people do end up leaving dentistry, and I respect that choice. But, no, you do not have to give up your career in order to be healthy.

The most important thing to remember about treating burnout is that you have to do something about it. Things will never resolve by being ignored; they'll only get worse until they're so bad they're unignorable. When I took action, I learned how to adjust things within myself and in my work. I found strategies that helped, and now I love going to work. You can, too. Now is the time to act. There is no better time to act than right here, right now.

Let's talk more about some of these stress factors and what you can do about it to turn your burnout around and get back to looking forward to going to work every day.

You can still have conflict at work. You can still have challenges at work. So I'm not saying that, you know, a breakthrough or success is when you walk into work and feel like: oh, this is the best job ever. I have no problems.

You can still have challenges, but it's how you deal with it, and you feel like you can deal with it. It feels like: okay, I can work on finding a solution here. It feels like: I can talk to management about this issue that I'm having. And you're not feeling that sense of desperation or that lack of hope that anything can change.

A very important indication of this sort of breakthrough is this sense of hope that's restored to life.

I mentioned how burnout could seep into other parts of life. Seeing people re-engage in things that they enjoy; hearing that people enjoy spending time with their kids again—I feel like those are breakthroughs.

It comes back to hope. I think when people are able to recapture a sense of hope, especially about what they can do, about positive changes they can make about things that aren't working right, either in the work setting or at home—I feel like that all points to a breakthrough.

–JEREMY SANTACROCE, RN/NP, LICSW

Key Takeaways

- Burnout isn't stress. Burnout is what you get when you've had unaddressed stress for too long.
- Burnout is a real thing with real symptoms.
- Burnout is very common among dentists.
- Burnout gets worse when it's ignored.
- There's hope! Take action now.

CHAPTER 2

DEPRESSION, ANXIETY, ADDICTION AND PAIN

The Hamster Wheel From Hell

The very first thing I ever said to my therapist was, "I wish I was an asshole who didn't care what others think."

I had walked into that office exhausted. I was mentally and physically tired of my job, tired of people, tired of feeling these feelings. I'm an introvert, so even at best, I don't love a lot of socializing. Socializing when I'm already tired is unimaginably exhausting. I found that the extroversion I had to pretend to in my dental practice was taking more and more energy all the time—I had to go from chair to chair, putting that happy face on, keeping my outward energy positive and high as inwardly I was crumbling from tension.

I dreaded staff functions and had started avoiding birthday parties and all the mental exhaustion they entailed. I simply did not have enough emotional gas in my tank to deal with a full day of pleasing patients and then socialize with staff after. I started racing home from work at the end of the day, every day, desperate for decompression.

That helped a little. But after a while, even that wasn't enough. I started to escape home at lunch to grab whatever time I could alone before having to return to the office I dreaded.

Finally, I realized that I could no longer avoid my office life. My nervousness, social anxiety, and exhaustion were not going away on their own; in fact, they were getting worse. I tried to envision the next thirty years of my career living like this and realized that I simply could not stay on this particular treadmill of unhappiness any longer. I had to take action.

When dentists describe their lives, they often use the same three words: stress, overwhelm, and dread. Does this sound familiar? You are not alone. In the 2015 Dentist Well-Being Survey report by the American Dental Association, 2,122 dentists described their stress levels and triggers. Over two-thirds of them, 79 percent, reported moderate to severe stress. More than a quarter of them, 26 percent, also reported moderate to high levels of depression.[2]

My Wake-Up Call

The therapist said, "Eric, you have anxiety."

Anxiety is something that I thought would never happen to me. I was always the easy-going one, the one who never got upset. Having problems was the thing I made sure never to do. I was a go-giver, not a go-getter. I knew that my patients, like many dental patients, brought their own fear and worry with them to the office, and it was my job to manage their anxiety, right?

Once my therapist pointed out the problem, I realized that what I thought was being laid-back was actually a lot of internally destructive people-pleasing and that it had been building for years.

---

[2] DentistryIQ. 2021. *How real dentists conquer real stress.* [online] Available at: <https://www.dentistryiq.com/practice-management/practice-management-tips/article/16367701/how-real-dentists-conquer-real-stress> [Accessed 28 February 2021].

DEPRESSION, ANXIETY, ADDICTION AND PAIN

First, it was a growing worry that I might not do a procedure perfectly and upset a patient so much that they might get upset, leave the office, or post a bad review. I started waking up at night, worrying about procedures I'd done.

Then I started worrying all the time about being sued. Every clinical procedure started to cause me greater anxiety. I was doing a lot of procedures that I didn't enjoy and wasn't comfortable with because I was anxious to keep the patient happy, the staff happy, and my bank happy.

As I kept pushing myself to do this, motivated by people-pleasing, my tolerance for doing even simple procedures started to diminish. I found myself incredibly nervous about previously simple procedures like inserting a crown or giving a mandibular nerve block injection, and constantly worried that even a small failure in clinical work would lead to displeasing the owner and staff and result in the loss of my job.

When things would go wrong, I'd lose sleep for nights, and my stomach lining tore itself up. I had spent years caring so much about what people thought of me that I swallowed my emotions, and as it turns out, swallowing emotions is an emotional repetitive stress injury. I'd developed anxiety.

My diagnosis was a total wake-up call. How I had been doing dentistry was causing me pain, and I needed to figure out how and why and how to keep it from happening again.

> *I've been working with healthcare professionals for sixteen years, and the burnout you're describing is what almost every physician, dentist, or pharmacist that I've worked with has experienced.*
>
> *Here's one thing we know: dentists are very smart people. They're very moral people, and they're very tough people. You wouldn't be in dentistry if you didn't have all three of those,*

and you couldn't even get through the education without all three.

So, clearly, what you presented was not a lack of those three. The territory that you lack is the capacity to deal with the emotional turmoil going on inside of a person who goes through her rigorous professional program and is spit out on the other side and then has to hire staff, run a business, and apply the craft.

If there's not big bandwidth inside the person's chest to deal with the emotional ramifications of that, then you have this thing called burnout.

You have a practitioner who has lived his or her entire life where it's all up to him or all up to her to use those three things: get smarter, get tougher, or get better. And this approach worked for almost everything, but it does not work with high levels of anxiety, depression, and burnout.

So often, anxiety is the accelerator. High octane people like dentists often have a hard time applying the brakes. What you described as burnout is actually an anxiety-depression loop.

–PHIL HERNDON MA, LPC-MHSP, NCC

Dentists in Pain

We're familiar with a patient-centered focus on how hard dentistry is for those who receive it, but it's also hard on those who provide it. Our profession often takes a toll, and statistics show that dentists experience several physical and emotional issues at a far higher rate than the general population.

Here are some alarming statistics:

DEPRESSION, ANXIETY, ADDICTION AND PAIN

- The suicide rate of dentists is more than twice the rate of the general population and almost three times higher than that of other white-collar workers.
- Emotional illness ranks third in order of frequency of health problems amongst dentists, while in the general population, it ranks tenth.
- Coronary disease and high blood pressure are over 25 percent more prevalent among dentists than in the general population.
- Dentists suffer psycho-neurotic disorders at a rate of two and a half times greater than physicians.
- The number one killer of dentists is stress-related cardiovascular disease.
- The dental profession in North America loses the numerical equivalent of one large dental school class each year.[3]

According to the *American Dental Association's* (ADA) 2015 Health and Wellness Survey, a total of 11 percent of dentists surveyed were diagnosed with depression, 6 percent were diagnosed with an anxiety disorder, and 4 percent were suffering from panic attacks. A total of 28 percent of dentists involved in the study reported seeking help for their mental health, while 44 percent believed they could resolve their symptoms without seeking professional help.

That's a lot of dentists who aren't getting their pain treated.

In this chapter, we're going to talk about the mental and physical wear and tear that can set us up for easy burnout and the different sources and manifestations of pain common to dentistry:

---

[3] Health-108, O., 2021. *Stress In Dentistry - It Could Kill You! - Oral Health Group*. [online] Oral Health Group. Available at: <https://www.oralhealthgroup.com/features/stress-in-dentistry-it-could-kill-you/> [Accessed 28 February 2021].

anxiety, depression, addiction, and chronic physical issues. We'll begin by talking about how we define pain, we'll talk about how it manifests, and we'll talk about solutions.

Pain: It's Not Just In Your Head

In this chapter, we're going to address physical and emotional pain together for these reasons:

It's all the same to our brains.

Research[4] shows that emotional pain activates the same areas of the brain that physical pain does. That is, rejection can literally feel like an attack on your heart. In these studies, test subjects were put into an fMRI, and they were given a picture of their ex and asked to think about their recent breakup.

The conclusion of this study was that you could use these pain processing areas' activation to accurately predict the presence of emotional pain 88 percent of the time. That is, emotional and physical pain are not only both equally distressing; they share the same areas in the brain. Rejection really does hurt.[5]

Here's the part that most psychologizing tends to leave out: the brain is massively interconnected with the rest of the body. There

---

[4] Lieberman, M., 2021. *Does Rejection Hurt: An fMRI Study of Social Exclusion*. [online] Research Gate. Available at: <https://www.researchgate.net/profile/Matthew-Lieberman-3/publication/9056800_Does_Rejection_Hurt_An_fMRI_Study_of_Social_Exclusion/links/09e41508aa626460df000000/Does-Rejection-Hurt-An-fMRI-Study-of-Social-Exclusion.pdf> [Accessed 28 February 2021].

[5] Kross, E., Berman, M., Mischel, W., Smith, E. and Wager, T., 2011. *Social rejection shares somatosensory representations with physical pain*. [online] pnas.org. Available at: <https://www.pnas.org/content/108/15/6270.long> [Accessed 28 February 2021].

are direct neural connections via the brainstem and spinal cord. The circulatory and lymphatic systems also carry neurotransmitters (hormones and immune cells) that find receptor sites in the brain, which feedback and modulate the links between brain and body. In this way, every cell in the body—every cell—is linked into the nervous system and, as such, can be sensed and felt, whether or not we allow ourselves to be aware of this psychobiological fact.[6]

We, dentists, know the importance of pain relief and the danger of letting pain go untreated. There is still a stigma around emotional pain that it's not real and that we should just compartmentalize it away in order to do our jobs, but these findings show how serious and real emotional pain can be and how dangerous it is to neglect whatever is hurting.

This is important because the pain of rejection, and the fear people have of this pain, is at the core of many of the poor coping patterns we get into as dentists. Fear of rejection leads to people-pleasing and poor boundaries and communication. All three of those behaviors contribute to bad management and toxic work culture that burns everyone out. Solving for burnout means tracking these behaviors to their source: pain.

Chronic pain of one kind will often lead to a chronic experience of the other. People who experience debilitating back pain will often develop depression, and anxiety often manifests through physical ailments like chest pain. If you have one, you'll often end up with the others. This becomes an increasingly destructive feedback loop, both because the presence of depression increases the

---

[6] Fogel, A., 2012. *Emotional and Physical Pain Activate Similar Brain Regions.* [online] Psychology Today. Available at: <https://www.psychologytoday.com/us/blog/body-sense/201204/emotional-and-physical-pain-activate-similar-brain-regions> [Accessed 28 February 2021].

risks of getting sick and dying but also because studies show that having one kind of pain will sometimes keep the other from being adequately treated.

The presence of a chronic medical illness may reduce the likelihood that physicians or other health care providers recognize or treat depression. The demands of chronic illness management may crowd concerns of depression out of the visit agenda. Providers may also not look beyond a chronic medical illness to explain nonspecific symptoms, such as fatigue or poor concentration. Even when they recognize symptoms of depression, they may defer treatment, believing that "anyone would be depressed" in such a situation.[7]

My friend Phil Herndon MA, LPC-MHSP, NCC runs a rehab center that treats dentists and other professional clinicians for emotional and addiction recovery.

> *"Yes, chronic pain is real. Bessel van der Kolk wrote a seminal work on how anxiety and physiology tie together. When we become anxious, our temperature goes up; our breathing becomes more shallow. Sometimes we have topical hives, GI distress, joint pain. It's because the physiological body is holding all this stress.*
>
> *Then you take the 100 percent physiological thing—working bent over at weird angles all day long—and you add a level of burnout stress, and a physician or dentist can have a seventy-year-old body at age thirty-four because of the trauma it's holding."*
>
> —PHIL HERNDON MA, LPC-MHSP, NCC

---

[7] Simon GE. Treating depression in patients with chronic disease: recognition and treatment are crucial; depression worsens the course of a chronic illness. *West J Med.* 2001;175(5):292-293. doi:10.1136/ewjm.175.5.292

DEPRESSION, ANXIETY, ADDICTION AND PAIN

Whether our pain is emotional or physical doesn't matter to our brains. It's all felt in the same place. If you've treated someone who grinds their teeth or for TMD then you have seen how the emotional often becomes the physical. Those of us who've experienced chronic muscle or joint issues and repetitive injuries from chairside work know the emotional exhaustion that results from persistent physical pain. All pain is pain, and all pain needs to be treated. Your pain and your healing matter.

The pain is enough of a level that it affects every minute of my life, and you never get a vacation from it. It's mentally fatiguing. You almost try not to think about it too much, but I just want to get through each day because at the end of each day, I'm closer to the end of the week. Then I look forward to the upcoming holidays, cause I know there's only a couple of days then. Those weeks, they're marked on my calendar, and I'll go, all right, I'll get a little more time there. And it's not a little more time to lay on the couch. It's more like I got six days in a row here that I can be working on myself—stretching, strengthening, preparing myself for the next wave. It's a nonstop battle. It really is.

–ANONYMOUS

Why Are Dentists in Pain?

Dentistry puts us at high risk for developing both kinds of pain, emotional and physical.

One study examined the risks of 974 occupations and ranked dentistry as the second-most dangerous due to how dentistry exposes dental health care providers to disease, contaminants, and sitting, and how each of those exposure rates increases the risk of musculoskeletal disorders and colon cancer. [8]

Additionally, the way dentistry is structured and the kinds of people it attracts mean that dentists tend to be detail-oriented people who work in isolating and exhausting conditions.

Our profession has some built-in features that can help create pain or make painful things worse, and these are things we need to know in order to clearly see our own risk factors and create a proactive strategy for protecting our health.

Here are some of the features of dentistry that put us at greater risk:

We're isolated. Many dentists, especially in solo practices, are isolated from the support that naturally occurs among peers experiencing similar things. It's not like working in a big, varied medical practice or a hospital or office, where when it hits five o'clock, you can go out for a beer with your buddies and blow off steam, and this is twice as true since COVID-19 hit.

Additionally, the need to pay off student loans and the broader market have set us up seemingly in competition with one another. I think our real competition is whatever keeps our patients from getting in the chair or paying for treatment, but those who do see other dentists as adversaries instead of as potential peer support are that much more isolated.

Our job is built for pain. Dentistry is a profession of perfection and high expectations; trying to meet those standards every day while still being human can result in a lot of disappointment and frustration at best. We work hard to provide treatment that

---

[8] Kelsch, RDHAP, N., 2014. *Risks of Dentistry to Personal Health.* [online] Registered Dental Hygienist (RDH) Magazine. Available at: <https://www.rdhmag.com/pathology/oral-pathology/article/16404240/risks-of-dentistry-to-personal-health> [Accessed 28 February 2021].

is, ideally, painless, perfect, and long-lasting, when the reality is that dental treatment hurts, no treatment is perfect, and time and patient neglect can destroy what we've tried to build. As dentists, we have a complicated relationship with expectations of success and failure, and that can invite more emotional pain.

We didn't learn another way in dental school. I don't know about you, but I got through dental school on adrenaline. My fear of failure helped me graduate, but that's a terrible long-term plan. When the anxiety was so bad that I burned out, I realized I had to switch to a different fuel, and that took a lot of learning and work. Dental school didn't teach us how to prevent and manage our own pain or how to resolve interpersonal issues that cause distress and arise from it.

Dentistry puts us in a tough position. As most of you probably know from painful experience, we dentists are at especially high risk for job-related musculoskeletal disorders. We labor for hours every day in static, awkward positions. We strain our eyes by staring at the same millimeter of space for minutes to hours at a time. We have to maintain steady hands and a light touch, even through long and complicated procedures, as we essentially perform surgery on awake, unrestrained patients. It's not surprising that this repeated workload results in damage to our bodies, especially our necks and backs.

Spending our life bent over people in pain would be emotionally and physically hard on anyone, but people who feel they need to do this perfectly and without asking for help are especially likely to develop serious pain.

We need to put on a happy face. Patients are coming to us for help, and many of them are already upset and anxious by the time they get in the chair. It's no secret people dread going to the dentist, and it's really draining to be feared or to have people see us as someone potentially causing them pain in their mouth and wallet. Who wants to be seen as the bad guy?

No one wants a dentist that's in a bad mood working on them. As dentists, we always have to be "on" and full of positive energy. Otherwise, patients may not feel calm and supported in the chair. As a result, we end up needing to be calm for two, and that's a lot of emotional labor. Nothing can make you unhappy faster than having to pretend you're happy.

We're stuck. The pressure to earn makes us keep grinding away without adequate rest. We work through our lunch breaks, on weekends, and miss vacations because of the pressure to do all-teeth-all-the-time.

It's ironic that a job focused on relieving and preventing the pain of others should end up causing so much pain to its practitioners. Again, I'm not sharing these observations in order to discourage anyone; far from it. I want to recognize these common issues and risk factors in order to help encourage those of us who feel they're struggling alone.

Manifestations of Pain

All pain is pain, and pain really hates to be ignored and neglected. That means sometimes pain manifests in less than ideal ways. Addiction is one of those ways—it's a disease some people develop when the pain becomes too much and is accompanied by secrecy and shame. Let's talk about this common problem.

Addiction

Addiction is a human problem, and dentists are definitely human. Dentists are at slightly higher risk for developing an addiction. "About 10 to 12 percent of the general population becomes addicted to alcohol or drugs at some point in their lives," says Michel A. Sucher, MD, medical director of the Arizona State Board of Dental Examiners' Monitored Aftercare Treatment Program. "For dentists and physicians, the prevalence is probably 12 to 19 percent."[9]

Why? Partly it's because of personality. Dentists, like other medical professionals, tend to have a compulsive personality type, which, like addicts, typically display behavior that is "anal retentive, compulsive-obsessive, controlling, and manipulative." These various patterns often allow addicts to find "enablers"—colleagues, employees, and family members—who allow drug dependencies to progress and worsen.

But, unlike many other medical professionals, dentists tend to be isolated in a single-practice setting, where they are in positions of authority and don't have a lot of supervision from colleagues. We, dentists, are exhausted by what we perceive as demands for perfection and constant emotional availability and have access to substances that the average non-medical professional doesn't. The same isolation and emotional exhaustion that create pain also lead people to seek any kind of pain relief.

> *Dentists have one of the highest suicide rates of any profession, as well as addiction rates. And it's because of the high levels of stress and the immediate access to certain types of medications that are easily abusable and highly addictive. So, yeah, it's always been a concern with the dental clients that I've worked with.*
>
> –DR. ALDEN CASS

---

[9] Curtis, DDS, MAGD, E., 2011. *When Dentists Do Drugs: A Prescription for Prevention*. [online] Dentistwellbeing.com. Available at: <http://www.dentistwellbeing.com/pdf/DentistsDoDrugs.pdf> [Accessed 28 February 2021].

Addiction: Signs

It can be hard to know when we've developed an addiction to something because addictions can build gradually over time. This is because addiction is a chronic disease that affects our brain's reward, motivation, and memory functions. Stress, depression, anxiety, and other forms of pain can affect those functions, too, which can predispose someone to develop addictions.

Addictions can be to substances (nicotine, alcohol, inhalants, medications, or other drugs) or behaviors (gambling, gaming, sex, working, shopping, using the Internet, or social media).

Early warning signs of addiction include:

- experimentation with substances or other vices
- family history of addiction
- being particularly drawn to an activity or substance
- seeking out situations where the substance or activity is present
- episodes of binging or loss of control with little to no feelings of remorse after

It can be hard to know when someone has an addiction versus when they're just socially drinking, smoking, or gaming. Some habits can be okay in moderation but drive a person to dependency if they're using them to cope with extreme stress and pain. When habits become addictions, people experiencing the addiction will often manifest the following changes in their physical, emotional, and social health:

- a lack of interest in hobbies or activities that used to be important
- neglecting relationships or reacting negatively to those closest to them
- missing important obligations like work

DEPRESSION, ANXIETY, ADDICTION AND PAIN

- risk-taking tendencies, especially to get drugs or continue certain behaviors
- ignoring the negative consequences of their actions
- a distinct change in sleeping patterns that result in chronic fatigue
- increased secrecy, like lying about the amount of substance used or time spent
- constant illness
- unexplained injuries
- an abrupt change in weight
- increased tolerance to drugs
- memory loss or problems with recall
- sudden changes in mood
- aggressive behavior
- irritability
- depression
- apathy

> *In the addiction world, we call the synthetic chemicals "temporary anesthesia," emotional Novocaine. Dentists inject this emotional Novocaine through alcohol, acting out sexually, gambling, addiction, benzos, opiates—it's all pain relief.*
>
> *You probably know this as a scientist, but when spectrometer scans came along, they discovered that emotional pain and physical pain are processed in the same part of the limbic brain. The limbic brain doesn't know the difference between the two.*
>
> *Think about the euphemisms we use when we're emotionally hurt: kicked in the gut, stabbed in the back, doubled over, broke my heart. We intuitively used examples*

of physical pain to describe emotional pain, and it turns out they're processed in the same place.

That's the reason people take opiates when they break their ankle and opiate when they're depressed, stressed, or burned out. The opiate receptors in the limbic brain feel it all as the same pain.

And so you have a lot of opiate-addicted dentists and healthcare providers because they hurt. They experienced constant criticism, constantly boxed stuff up, and then talk to the next patient like nothing happened. It all catches up to them, and their limbic brain goes, I need opiates. I don't care if it's a broken leg or a broken heart—I need opiates.

–PHIL HERNDON MA, LPC-MHSP, NCC

Addiction: Solutions

Addiction affects all of a person's life, and a person often needs to make changes in their entire life in order to recover from addiction.

Reversing the conditions that lead to the development of addictions can help with recovering from them, too.

Admit you have a problem. It's common for addicts to understate the seriousness of their condition or to deny it entirely. There's help for addiction, and admitting there's a problem is the first step towards real recovery.

Get treatment. There are options for getting free of addiction. Consider whether inpatient rehab, outpatient rehab, twelve-step programs, or a combination of the above are right for you. Find a therapist you trust and get honest with them. Make sure you get to the root of the pain that leads you to seek this behavior in the first place.

Get support. Addiction thrives on isolation, secrecy, and shame. The best way to defeat that is to connect with people—friends, family, other dentists, other people struggling with addiction. Make sure you spend time with people who will support your recovery instead of enabling your addiction.

Build new boundaries. Find new hobbies, set new life goals, and put boundaries in place between yourself and access to the substances or behaviors that encourage compulsive, self-destructive behaviors.

Progress, not perfection. The desire for perfection and control causes pain that encourages addiction. You will likely relapse. Make recovery plans that you can follow while being an imperfect yet worthy human.

Depression: Signs

There are many symptoms of depression that overlap with burnout. Here's the rundown of how you may feel run down:

- persistent sadness
- loss of interest and pleasure, especially in things you used to enjoy
- sleep change (way more or less than previously)
- appetite change (way more or less than previously)
- fatigue and exhaustion
- poor concentration, inability to focus, forgetfulness
- mood swings
- numbness
- anger
- increased use of substances like alcohol
- thoughts of suicide*

Something important to remember about depression is that it can look very different in different people. If the people at your office seem especially irritating lately, it's possible that you're experiencing depression.

For me, depression showed up as a total loss of motivation to do dental work. I lost all that drive that took me through dental school and into practice.

I also noticed that my treatment planning style changed. I started watching more suspicious areas instead of treating them because I felt like I didn't have the energy to do the treatment.

For some people, depression feels like an increasing emotional distance and numbness, and in the context of burnout, that actually makes a lot of sense. If we feel pain from caring too much—caring about what people think of us, caring about our clinical skills being perfect, caring about difficult debt load and business management—it makes sense that our brains will try to protect us from the threat of caring too much by making us go numb. We're dentists, and we know all about the value of blocking pain.

But the natural anesthesia of emotional numbness and burnout isn't a long-term solution, and if you ignore it, it'll only lead to increased harm. Please, reach out now.

The two most common reasons I hear from dentists who don't want to seek therapy:

One is fear, "It won't help."

Two is, "I'm already busy."

I get it. They don't have another paradigm. They look at it as something they have to do, not something they're investing in.

Dentists and other professionals could see it as investing in their career and life—not just adding something to a to-do list, but getting an outlet that will make you a better dentist.

You become a better dentist because you're fresher, more available. It's not necessarily that you repair or extract teeth better, but there's more self to bring to patients—new limbic resonance, which allows for better personal care.

Start your career by getting the help you need as an investment in being able to have a life in your profession.

–PHIL HERNDON MA, LPC-MHSP, NCC

Depression: Solutions

Reach out for help. Mental health and dental health are alike in that regular maintenance is something we can handle on our own, but the big issues need expert help. It's all too common for dentists to believe they can handle this themselves, but please get in touch with a professional.

Again, pain is pain. You wouldn't leave a torn rotator cuff or an abscess untreated, right? Your brain is like a muscle, and you need to exercise it just like you would your biceps at the gym. Seeing a therapist and/or life coach is exercise for your brain and much-needed treatment for your pain.

The earlier, the better. Every dentist that I have talked to who has sought professional advice said the same thing: they wish they'd done it much sooner.

We focus so much on improving our dentistry by taking CE courses or changing our practices to help our patients more, but what about helping yourself? Investing in your health will help your patients the most in the long term because when we're in pain, crashing and burning isn't a matter of if, but when.

Get help with assessment. The thing about emotional issues is that sometimes the very problem that characterizes our pain also keeps us from clearly discerning our problem. Ask someone you trust, who has your best interests at heart, if you've changed lately. Listen to them. If they say you have, write down what they say, and bring it with you to any counseling appointments.

The most unrealistic expectation is to believe that ignoring depression will somehow make it go away. There's a tendency for people in the middle of depression to believe that things can't get better, but a combination of therapy, medication, and lifestyle changes can substantially improve your standard of living—and you're worth that.

> *I know it takes a lot of courage to reach out to someone, especially if it's your first time into treatment.*
>
> –JEREMY SANTACROCE, RN/NP, LICSW

Anxiety

Here are some ways anxiety may look and feel:

- Worry and fear
- Sense of impending doom
- Insomnia
- Headaches
- Nausea
- Racing pulse
- Chest pains
- Hypervigilance and restlessness
- Irritability and anger
- Mood swings
- Fatigue

DEPRESSION, ANXIETY, ADDICTION AND PAIN

- Sweating
- Difficulty in focusing
- Racing or unwanted thoughts
- Persistent worry
- Palpitations
- Trembling

And, not to scare you, but please remember that cardiovascular disease is the number one killer of dentists, so if you're experiencing any of these symptoms, go get checked out by your doctor.

A major contributor to my burnout was how my anxiety fed my people-pleasing impulses. Phil Herndon MA, LPC-MHSP, NCC calls this an "approval addiction." A key part of my recovery was seeing that connection and making the needed changes in myself and my work so that I could get comfortable in my own skin and my own life.

Something else that dentists need to keep in mind regarding anxiety is that many of us have found its adrenaline-based energy spikes useful. Dental school is really challenging and very competitive, and it's not unusual for dental school students to rely on anxiety to give them that extra bolus of energy to make it through another exam.

This was how I got through college and dental school: I relied on my fear of failure to get me through. This worked to help me graduate, but then it turned on me once I moved into the real world. The demands of dentistry poured gasoline on the fires lit by my fears, and I was burnt to a crisp.

Again, the problem with anxiety is that it's sort of a hormonal repetitive stress injury. It's not a long-term solution for managing our focus, motivation, or performance. If that sounds like you, it might be time to explore different methods of self-motivation that aren't as corrosive to your long-term health.

> *My least favorite part about going to work every day is the stress from patients when they aren't comfortable.*
>
> *My practice is based on making people comfortable. When people aren't, it sucks. Our industry fricking sucks for people. I'm still doing all the cleanings, and when I hit a sensitive spot—when, at any moment, there might be a shooting pain? I am upset from people being uncomfortable, and I wish I were doing something that people could relax and enjoy.*
>
> *So, instead, I'm tense. I take on a lot of that tension, and it's the same with their emotional stress. I take that on as well.*
>
> –ANONYMOUS

Anxiety Solutions

Take care of your heart!

The psychological stress of working with apprehensive and fearful patients can be devastating to the dental practitioner. There is now considerable evidence that dentists experience patterns of physiological stress responses (increased heart rate, high blood pressure, sweating, etc.) that parallel the patient's responses when performing dental procedures that evoke patient fear and anxiety. This, in turn, can lead to an early heart attack for the dentist.[10]

Get yourself checked out. If you're having palpitations and trouble breathing, get your cardiovascular health checked. And if that looks fine, you're still not off the hook—your body wouldn't be having that distress if it weren't in some kind of pain. If the professionals you're

---

[10] Health-108, O., 2021. *Stress In Dentistry - It Could Kill You! - Oral Health Group.* [online] Oral Health Group. Available at: <https://www.oralhealthgroup.com/features/stress-in-dentistry-it-could-kill-you/> [Accessed 28 February 2021].

seeing think medication is a good idea, please be open to it. Physical symptoms in the body sometimes need physical solutions.

Address anxious behaviors

In my case, I needed to address the people-pleasing that was at the root of my increasingly unmanageable anxiety. When my therapist helped me see the pattern of how I constantly sacrificed my happiness to try to preserve the happiness of others, I was able to make changes in how I approached office management and creating rapport with patients. I'm happy to say that now I am able to present treatment to a patient without being deeply invested in whether they like me or agree to my plan—thanks to working with my therapist and shifting my work priorities.

However, it didn't happen overnight. It took a lot of time and work on my part—I did a lot of soul-searching as I made significant changes in my practice.

Refer out

I'm all for people working diligently on increasing their clinical skills, focusing on generating revenue, and trying new things, but for me, I realized that the positives of trying to do procedures I didn't enjoy were outweighed by the negatives. Now I refer those out or delegate to a coworker—life's too short to hate your job.

Case selection is a lifesaver. It includes clinical procedures that hurt me to do and patients who aren't a good fit for my practice. Saying "no" to both of these stressors helped me say "yes" to myself and my own healing and happiness. I'm not doing the procedure and not generating revenue; however, by not doing the procedure, I'm generating mental currency I call "Blocky (enter your last name here) Bucks."

Switch to an alternative fuel

Running on the adrenaline spikes that anxiety provides is how some people get by, especially if they're feeling dragged down by depression or are dealing with something like ADHD. That adrenaline flame got me through school but burned me out in the real world. There is no way I could have kept up that adrenaline-based lifestyle for another thirty years.

If you used your anxiety to propel you through college and dental school or through regular life, act now to take steps towards figuring that out and switching to a fuel tank that's less likely to burn you out. The goal here is to find a way to enjoy work for the long haul without hurting ourselves in the process.

> *The most common obstacles to dentists seeking mental health care include social stigma, feeling like it takes too much time, and perhaps a sense of shame or a feeling of "I should just try harder." That a person just has to push through, that pushing through will make it fine.*
>
> *Maybe a lack of understanding of what mental health treatment involves. Maybe a worry of what your colleagues or friends might think if they find out you're talking to a therapist.*
>
> *Maybe there's a feeling of being stuck, that nothing's going to change, so why bother? How is a pill going to make me any happier? I don't know how going and talking to someone is going to change any of this. I don't know how a pill is going to make me any happier.*
>
> *I think that there's even fear because if I find out that this job is really tough and that I need to rethink my approach to it, that can be really scary. That change can be scary. Many of us would prefer to stay in our patterns rather than challenge what we're doing and think about other ways of being.*
>
> –JEREMY SANTACROCE, RN/NP, LICSW

DEPRESSION, ANXIETY, ADDICTION AND PAIN

Physical Pain

About ten years ago, I tore my labrum. There was no traumatic incident. I just started to develop this deep pain in my left shoulder that persisted until it started affecting my sleep. It could have been from years of weight lifting or tennis, but the years of wear and tear from the dentistry grind certainly didn't help. Like many other dentists, by that time, I'd spent ten years doing what so many of us do—holding static, awkward positions for several hours a day, several days a week. The constant holding of a position and poor ergonomics takes a toll on the body.

The only thing worse than hurting yourself with the physical demands of dentistry is having to meet the physical demands of dentistry when you're already injured. To put it mildly, working while in pain is not fun—it's mentally exhausting!

Growing up, I've never had health issues. Never had muscle aches or pains, and I played sports. My whole life, I never had a problem. Never had a problem in dental school.

And then, I was working the easy forty hours and, you know, I was hungry. "Emergencies? Put them in my lunch!" "I'll work late." You know, all of that. I was very productive.

And then, at some point, I just started to get a little stiff. I noticed sleeping wasn't so comfortable. I have a friend who's a physical therapist who was unofficially helping me out. And then it escalated. One early summer day, years ago, I went to pick something up, and everything kind of went at once.

I had full spasms—neck, shoulder, back kind of hips. I don't know if you've ever had an official spasm, almost like when you pinch a nerve, and you can't move, but it was scary.

I didn't know what was going on. I've never had that. I went to doctors and doctor after doctor, and they said there didn't seem to be anything wrong. That they didn't see anything, that I should go do some physical therapy.

So I did the rounds: physical therapy, ice, massage, acupuncture. I tried everything, you know? The self-help stuff. I take some statins which have been linked to muscle pain, so I took myself off the statins, but nothing really made a difference. I had multiple MRIs, multiple steroid shots for set joint blocks, spinals—everything.

I do have a couple of small pinched nerves and discs, but those are very specific. I have a lot of general muscle pain and cramping and tightness, extreme tightness. When I get up in the morning, I can't put socks on. It takes me forever to get going. I have to be very careful.

And like I said, I've been through multiple rounds of physical therapy, and there's not a specific diagnosis. I've been checked for arthritis, and other autoimmune issues, and ankylosing spondylitis; I mean, I've been looked at by everyone, and they kind of go, eh, we don't really know.

But it seems like, in general, according to the various therapists I've seen, I do tend to have very tight musculature, but I also have very loose joints.

So I think it's just the perfect combination of a bad job for my little personal idiosyncrasies. And if I was doing something else, it may not have ever manifested. This job just puts you in a bad position.

–ANONYMOUS

Dentists are more likely to get injured on the job and yet less likely to seek treatment. According to an ADA study, 92 percent of dentists keep working even if they have physical pain, and most do not seek a physician's help. For example, of the dentists diagnosed with arthritis, 84 percent failed to seek treatment. The main reason they gave for not seeking treatment for physical and mental stress was their belief that a dentist should be able to solve problems without help.[11]

Poor ergonomics is a major issue for dentists. The ADA Council of Dental Practice's Dental Wellness Advisory Committees surveyed dentists' well-being and found that two-thirds of the respondents reported that they suffered from neck pain and nearly half of them said that it was either moderate or severe in its intensity. A similar percentage reported low back pain, and again, half of those surveyed said that it ranged from moderate to severe.[12]

Being a dentist can literally be a pain in the neck. Here are some of the things that can make doing dentistry cause more pain than it should:

- Improper placement of patient chairs, which removes easy access to the patient's mouth and alters the dentist's seated posture.
- Bending, twisting, and holding awkward poses during treatment.
- Poor intraoral lighting—this encourages the dentist to perch on the edge of their stool as they peek into the oral cavity.
- Dental stools or chairs that are unstable or hard to adjust or somehow make the dentist have to sit askew on the chair to compensate for its deficiencies.

---

[11] DentistryIQ. 2021. *How real dentists conquer real stress.* [online] Available at: <https://www.dentistryiq.com/practice-management/practice-management-tips/article/16367701/how-real-dentists-conquer-real-stress> [Accessed 28 February 2021].

[12] Ada.org. 2018. *ADA Wellness Survey reveals dentists' ergonomic issues.* [online] Available at: <https://www.ada.org/en/publications/ada-news/2018-archive/january/ada-wellness-survey-reveals-dentists-ergonomic-issues> [Accessed 28 February 2021].

- Instruments that are hard to grip or aren't properly sharpened and require more exertion in order to be effective.

> *It was frightening at first, painful. Every other injury I've ever had in my life, eventually, I got past it, and it would go away. This has never gone away. It never got better.*
>
> *I've got multiple types of chairs and saddle stools. I've tried all of those. I've attended ergonomic courses, and they'll say, "Oh, you've got to do this or that." And none of it seems to touch a lot of what I'm doing.*
>
> *When I have a tough angle, or during certain things I'm doing, I stand less. I'll do less of the craning over and just stand. I try not to sit in one spot all the time. If I'm having access to one area, I'll sit, but—even mid-procedure—I'll stand up and kind of elbow my assistant out of the way and say, I'm coming over.*
>
> *That's not too bad on the short stuff. It's the long ones that are hard. Particularly the procedures where you can't take a breath, where you can't let anything get wet, where there's a limited amount of time. At least with a crown prep or something, you can leave part way through, and it's not going to change anything. But doing a quadrant of resins is very, very bad for me.*
>
> *It's hard work to work in this little tiny space on a moving target upside down or trying to be friendly and jovial. I don't think it's an easy job; it's very difficult. I'm more of an introvert too, so it takes a lot of juice for me to be a friendly guy, constantly reassuring and calming, while at the same time having pain and sitting there.*
>
> *In longer procedures, I can feel certain things cramping up and tightening. I have a hard time taking a break from it. I don't know how to slack off. I'm no hero, but I can't say,*

well, my back hurts, so I'm just going to do this faster or not do it at all.

I feel like I sacrifice myself, and I kind of hate myself for it. I kinda hate the job for it. You can't really do this job part way.

It's mentally and physically exhausting to get home and have pain and not feel well, to not want to get on the floor with the kids, to not sleep well. And then you wake up the next morning, and it's like stubbing your toe. You just keep doing it, and you have to do it every day, multiple times a day. You have to do it to yourself, knowing what you're getting into.

It's fatiguing. It's exhausting. It's been tough just to keep a positive lookout, even on other aspects of life, because it feels like you're in this rut where it's never going to end.

–ANONYMOUS

Pain: Solutions

Call your doctor

Studies show that this is really hard for dentists like us. As a group, we often don't ask for help. As a group, we're also really unhealthy. Let's change that.

If you have emotional pain, call your doctor and find a therapist. If you have physical pain, again, call your doctor and find a physical therapist. Avail yourself of whatever resources will help—massage, exercise, acupuncture, chiropractic, medication, and other needed medical procedures, like surgery.

Stop pain before it starts

Figure out your ergonomics—there are consultants you can call who can help you assess your risks and solutions. Have a staff member photograph or video your posture and how you hold your instruments so you can get a better understanding of what may be hurting you and help properly fit you for helpful devices like loupes.

Take care of yourself outside the office because dentistry is a contact sport, and you need both protective equipment and good judgment. For me, that means I don't go skiing or mountain biking with my friends because I feel they're too risky. If I hurt my wrist or hand, I could be out of a job for an extended period, and it's just not worth it.

Recalibrate your work/life balance: the sweatpants to scrubs equilibrium theory

What can you do to improve your life both in the office and away from the office? We spend the majority of our waking hours at our offices, so we need to make sure we make the best of both. It's important to leave after a long day physically; it's equally important to leave at the end of the day mentally, too. The goal here is to get back to looking forward to going into work, and you can't do that if you haven't left yet!

I created a theory for myself to help balance my work/life. It's called: The Sweatpants to Scrubs Equilibrium. My life revolves around either wearing sweatpants or scrubs, and it works like this: My scrubs represent the hustle. While comfortable, they are what I wear when I'm in "go" mode. Dr. Block is ON when he's in his scrubs. They also represent my work mindset. When I'm in my scrubs, I'm thinking about work and only work—versus my sweatpants. My sweatpants are what I wear when I'm in chill mode.

That means I wear them to work in the morning and only change out of them when I'm ready to work for the day. I also put them on as soon as I get home. They represent relaxation, family, "me time," and a no-hustle mentality. For a while, when I was in my scrubs, I couldn't wait to escape into the comfort of my sweatpants—both physically and mentally. I hated going to work. I wanted to be a full-time sweat-pants guy. I also struggled with the converse. I would physically be wearing my sweatpants, but my mind was in "scrub-mode," constantly worried about work.

Now, I'm now able to go 100 percent in my scrubs at work and then 100 percent for my family and me when it's time for the sweatpants. This shift didn't happen overnight; I had to work on setting boundaries and fixing things at the office so it wouldn't be a place I worried about or wanted to escape from.

There are three rules that I reference when talking about this back and forth battle, and I call them the rules of Sweatpants Fight Club, that if you adopt, you will feel much more balanced.

The first 1st rule of Sweatpants Fight Club: you must realize there is a problem

Unlike the movie with Brad Pitt, you must talk about it. You need to look at yourself in the mirror and ask yourself if you enjoy going to work every day. Are you happy?

The 2nd rule of Sweatpants Fight Club: get help

We all need help. Many dentists and hygienists are solitary, but we don't have to be.

I took action to get the help I needed. I picked up the phone and finally called a therapist. I also started engaging more with my peers. Asking for help is hard but so worth it.

The 3rd and most important rule of Sweatpants Fight Club: get comfortable on the inside

You need to get comfortable in your own skin. Personally, I used to sacrifice my own happiness for the sake of others because I wanted to avoid confrontation. I wasn't comfortable enough to say no because I didn't want to disappoint anyone. I wanted everyone to like me. Along with therapy and coaching, I learned I had to take care of myself before taking care of others. This meant learning to say no, which to me meant saying yes to myself. And saying yes to myself helps me keep the sweats on.

What I've done to make my life outside work to say yes to myself are activities that help me totally forget about work. I got back into tennis, which puts me in kind of an awesome trance where I have so much fun that hours will go by in what feels like minutes. Those couple hours of being a bulldog on the court restore my daily zen. When I play, I don't think of dentistry or the office or staff or numbers or insurance. That mental break is key to recovering joy in dentistry and finding true sweatpants to scrubs equilibrium.

Make your office work for you

Is your clinical stool old and not offering enough support? Replace it. Could you use an armrest or better overhead light? Do you need to change your operatory layout? That could help with preventing a lot of pain, too.

Game Changer Alert: I stand now for all procedures, and my back pain has become insignificant. Sitting is the new smoking. In fact, I have completely removed the stools from all of my operatories. My assistants have also noticed a difference.

At my office, I've added areas and activities that support me in having a more pleasant work experience. I listen to music and podcasts to keep my brain in the zone.

My muscles get really tight, and the strain of chairside work exacerbates that, but yoga and hanging from a bar helps. I used to wait until the end of the day to run home or to a yoga class to finally get out the tightness and knots that piled up all day, but then I made my office even better by creating a little yoga studio in the back of my office so I can run in there between patients. There's a bar I can hang from, mats to stand on, massagers—it's a sanctuary, a home-away-from-home.

Now, it's just normal for me to talk to staff while in a yoga pose or hanging from a bar and do some quick sun salutations. My staff will come into my office, and I'm standing there with my stand-up desk and yoga mat in tree pose or warrior one, and we'll just continue on with the conversation like it's totally normal. I have an acupressure standing mat, a foam roller, and massagers there, too. Knowing I have a spot dedicated to keeping me healthy goes a long way towards helping me look forward to going to work every day. You don't need to wait until your eight-hour work day is over to stretch or decompress. I am constantly doing this throughout the day and in between patients.

Speak up

People-pleasing kept me silent when I was suffering. I used to not want to keep pestering the patient by moving their head or opening their mouth. So I would sacrifice my own physical position to accommodate them.

Addressing my anxiety helped me change this behavior and say NO to suffering needlessly in silence and YES to my health.

Now, instead, I use the Isolite or VacuLUX isolation mouth props and constantly move the patient's head around to accommodate my position. Remember, they are in an uncomfortable position for a few minutes—we are in uncomfortable positions for thirty years. I will often direct the patient to lift their chin like they are looking at the ceiling and tip their head to the right so I can access the second molars. Small shifts like this make an incredible difference.

Address the stress

I read a book by Dr. Sarno called *The Mind Body Connection*, which suggested a connection between the emotional distress I was accumulating as an anxious dentist and the pain in my back.

It took me years to conquer that stress and anxiety. I had to get confident in myself and my skills and train my brain to reassure me that I was doing my best and that if something goes wrong—like if a filling pops out or a crown needs to be redone, or a patient has pain—that I can deal with it if and when it happens.

Sure I get stiff and have back pain here and there, but it is minimal and doesn't affect my day like it used to. And part of that is due to physical changes I made in my workspace, but I think it's also due to the internal and emotional changes I made. I took my pain seriously and did something about it.

> *People who've not been in therapy might think that therapy is this:*
>
> *I go in. I talk to someone, they tell me what to do.*
>
> *Therapy is actually the exact opposite of that. They're not supposed to tell you what to do. The therapist is supposed to help you figure out what to do.*
>
> *So for me, what I really enjoy is witnessing and being part of that journey of self-discovery. I enjoy seeing that person making positive changes in their life that they've been trying to achieve. I love seeing people figure out ways through their challenges.*

DEPRESSION, ANXIETY, ADDICTION AND PAIN

> *I personally have a couple of ways that I might handle a situation, but then, in helping someone think about their options, they may come up with a completely different way of handling a situation that even I hadn't thought of.*
>
> *My work—it's really rewarding to see people persevere in some pretty challenging times.*
>
> —JEREMY SANTACROCE, RN/NP, LICSW

Key Takeaways

- All pain is pain. Emotional pain and physical pain—it's all brain pain. Do whatever you can to address the sources of your pain. Don't try to ignore it; it'll just get worse. It won't go away on its own, but it can be treated.
- The apathy of depression is actually a protective mechanism. Your brain is numbing you out because you're in pain. Make some changes in your life, so your brain doesn't feel so threatened by feelings that it numbs you out.
- Anxiety is super uncomfortable, but it's also common and treatable. If you're feeling the symptoms listed here, reach out and get help.
- Addiction is fed by shame. If your life is changing and you're withdrawing, take a look at your coping mechanisms and know that you can get help and that you're not alone.
- Fix your work-life balance by finding ways to leave dentistry at the office mentally and physically. You can't look forward to going to work if you never leave it in the first place.
- Find your yoga, whether it's actually yoga or not. Do what you need to do to decompress from the day-to-day grind of dentistry.

- Make your office a welcoming place to be that is geared towards preserving your mental and physical health.
- Finally, if you're having thoughts of despair or self-harm, please talk to someone.

Suicide Hotline Number
National Suicide Prevention Lifeline
Hours: Available 24 hours.
800-273-8255

CHAPTER 3

PEOPLE-PLEASING AND CONFLICT RESOLUTION

Dental school helped us practice our clinical skills, but we learned little to nothing about communication, work culture, or how to manage our own expectations and emotions as we experience the stresses, frustrations, and rejections that are all a part of everyday life in a dental practice.

Especially as an associate in a practice, I felt like I needed to please everyone—everyone but me. I put myself last so that everyone else could take precedence. I wanted everyone to like me, so I said yes to everything. "Yes, I'll call the patient about that problem!" "Yes, I'll call the lab." I wanted to make the staff happy. I wanted to make my boss happy. I especially wanted to make patients happy, both because helping people is half the point of dentistry but also because that would help me earn an income and their approval.

What I absolutely didn't want was a confrontation. I would do anything to avoid that. I would go to the front office to manage some scheduling and find myself asking, "Okay, when you're done with that magazine, can you do this for me?" (I wish I were kidding here.)

Saying "NO" as an associate is very difficult, especially if, like me, you're an introverted people-pleaser. All decisions, actions, and boundaries are often harder as an associate. Why?

You need the money. As associates, we're in debt up to our eyeballs. Our only chance of paying that back is to keep our jobs in dental practices, and being seen as unproductive and the squeaky wheel seems to contradict that goal.

You don't have authority. Many associates join practices where not only are the owners more experienced, but the staff is too. They regard associates as junior dentists or just another member of the team. The difficulties here compound if the practice doesn't have a clear chain of command or excellent accountability. It means you have to rely on trial and error to understand the unspoken flowchart governing the practice, and that is a really disempowering experience. It means that you can't order staff to do their jobs or bring consequences to bear; you are stuck in the position of supplicant. Most of the time, we don't know the actual culture of the office until we've been there a few months.

You don't know your limits. Associates are still learning so much—about clinical skills and applied business management, about which procedures they like or dislike, which patients they connect with well or not at all. It's not hard to over-promise when you're still fulfilling your potential, and in the well-intentioned zeal to learn and accumulate experience, associates may agree to too much—difficult cases, difficult patients, maybe even difficult offices—and find themselves exhausted and unable to follow through as they'd hoped.

By the way, not knowing your limits is nothing to be ashamed of. It doesn't show a lack of ability or intelligence, only a lack of experience. It's something all dentists go through at one point or another, so try to make the best of the experience by accepting the things you learn about yourself and use that to correct course as you keep moving.

You're anxious. There are a lot of things we likely fear as we begin our careers, things like letting patients down, upsetting staff,

PEOPLE-PLEASING AND CONFLICT RESOLUTION

disappointing owners, or failing a procedure so badly the patient leaves the practice, files a complaint with the dental board, or worse ... sues us. Excessive people-pleasing and lack of boundaries is a way we bargain with that fear.

You're new to teams. Dentistry is demanding and collaborative work. By the time we graduate from dental school, we've had years of focusing on our individual achievements in a competitive setting, only to then enter an environment where we're part of a continuing group project, where we need to help real people who may be in pain. We are a cog in the practice's wheel and don't want to be the broken part that derails the office. That's stressful!

For many people, this is kind of an introvert's nightmare, and we may be new to the things that keep groups healthy and balanced—the respectful give-and-take of boundaries. But it takes experience and sometimes even specific training to learn how to make and maintain boundaries, and in order to do so, we have to address our fear of conflict.

> *The people-pleasing you're describing is classic codependency, or, for lack of a better term, approval addiction. It comes from a really deep well, and so much of that has to do with our stories.*
>
> *And I don't mean parental blame—even just being in your own story because so much of codependency has to do with making sure I don't get abandoned. I don't want my patients to abandon me. I don't want colleagues to abandon me. I want people to respect me and like me and keep coming back for my services. I want to know I've been of service.*
>
> *People will do remarkable things, go to remarkable lengths to keep from being abandoned, and that's so tied to where we come from. If we're paying attention, we see how terrifying it is for people to, well, fill in the blank: reject me,*

abandon me, humiliate me, not want to be my friend, not want to be my patient.

Frozen terror so often becomes anxiety and starts that loop of "I need something that will help me not feel this anxiety." So I might go to synthetic medication and become overly dependent. I might work myself to death and have an addiction to approval, to keep from being abandoned, and get into that anxiety-depression loop.

–PHIL HERNDON MA, LPC-MHSP, NCC

People-Pleasing Leads To Resentment and Burnout

When I was an associate, I had major imposter syndrome. The dictionary defines imposter syndrome as: "A psychological condition that is characterized by persistent doubt concerning one's abilities or accomplishments accompanied by the fear of being exposed as a fraud despite evidence of one's ongoing success."[13]

My Imposter Syndrome helped create a situation where I was increasingly isolated and afraid. Because I felt like I needed to be something I wasn't in order to please others, I couldn't afford to acknowledge or communicate my feelings or needs—my fear, my exhaustion, my deep introverted need for silent downtime so I could recharge. My willingness and ability to communicate suffered, and I didn't know what to do to change a situation that was becoming increasingly toxic to my health.

I was already always trying to do my best and already always nervous I wasn't living up to that standard. Then I became nervous

---

[13] https://www.merriam-webster.com/dictionary/impostor%20syndrome

PEOPLE-PLEASING AND CONFLICT RESOLUTION

all the time. My desire to please everyone led to a growing fear that shrank my clinical comfort zone. First, I backed away from procedures I probably could have learned just fine, and then I started to struggle with simple procedures that I'd previously had down pat. Even a simple restorative procedure or work on the lower molars felt threatening—I was constantly asking myself, "What if the patient wasn't numb enough? What if I caused them pain? Do they like me? Do they trust me? Do they trust my skills? Is the assistant on to me that I don't know what I'm doing?"

In my spinning exhaustion, a seemingly endless cycle began: I started to see patients differently. I lost my joy in the profession. Instead of seeing them as friends, or people I could help, I saw them as potential litigants, sources of distress, adversaries. Nothing I could do in the office would be enough, they were the enemy, and they couldn't be trusted. I crawled deeper into isolation and dreaded going to work every day.

Something had to change. I realized I needed to develop the emotional skills of managing fear, setting boundaries, and being honest in my communication.

People-pleasing had started as a way to manage my anxiety, but in the process, ironically became a fuel source for that same fear. This created a predictably exhausting situation as my anxiety flamed out of control as I burnt out.

I finally realized that where I was wasn't okay and that I needed to assess and address my situation so I could repair the damage these fears were doing to my mental health and my career. I hoped I could get back to a place where I could look forward to going to work every day.

Here are the strategies I've found helpful in moving into a more self-caring style of managing my own emotional experience around work:

Accept that it's a problem

It's a vulnerable thing to admit to being a people-pleaser because then addressing it means addressing the core experiences or fears that may have created this pattern in the first place. For many, this behavior shows up in their personal and professional lives in both subtle and profound ways. Take some time to think about why you're putting others before yourself. Make a list of who you put first and how that affects you. This can help you better notice when you're reflexively people-pleasing, so you can note the conditions that led to that response. That can give you insight into what needs to change internally and externally so that you can begin creating a new, better experience for yourself.

Get support

Reach out to peers, hire a life coach, work with a dental consultant, talk it over with a mentor, and go to therapy. Therapy is awesome, and my therapist has really helped me with managing my anxiety and changing my instinctive reaction people-pleasing into more balanced responses that are based on healthier boundaries. Personally, therapy and finding the right combination of medications were a great way to address my fear-driven behaviors at the source. They also helped me stop replaying the day's events, conversations, patient interactions, and situations over and over in my head. I used to obsess over the one or two mistakes or less than perfect outcomes rather than enjoy and celebrate the twenty positive outcomes.

Ask for and accept help

Those who seek to please often are more comfortable giving help than asking for it and accepting it, but it's that very imbalance that is so stressful. Start small if you need, and try asking a colleague or a team member to help you with a task or to take it over entirely. Remember, the first time is often the hardest; after that, it'll get easier each time. The great thing about this strategy is how effective it is at addressing what people-pleasing, imposter syndrome, anxiety, and burnout all have in common: a feeling of isolation. When others are helping you, you know you're not alone, and you don't have to do everything by yourself.

Practice saying "No."

I was terrified that if I said "no," that people would be so upset, I'd lose the patient, revenue, or the staff would talk behind my back. My anxiety about never saying no was so constraining I contorted myself into knots to avoid it, which made me resent dentistry. What I discovered once I learned how to do it was that it wasn't the disaster I'd feared. Yes, some people pushed back, but I dealt with it, and you can, too. I kept this phrase in my head as I practiced saying "No": "Saying NO to them is saying YES to myself."

Practice accepting rejection

Dentistry is a profession where there will be an unavoidable amount of rejection. The sooner we can learn how to not take it personally, the better it will be for our mental health. The sooner you realize that dentistry is not all strawberries and cream like breakfast at Wimbledon.

Conflict is inevitable; prepare for it, so you don't have to fear it

Learn how to resolve conflict. It's a practicable skill that you can learn, and once you've been through conflict a few times and survived, you'll calm down more and more and be more willing to nip problems in the bud before they become big burnout-inducing issues.

> *I ended up getting into therapy. Between my therapist and a lot of soul-searing, I realized I needed to act.*
>
> *I was talking about being unhappy and it impeding my career, and she was trying to help me understand the one thing that makes us happy in careers and makes us feel fulfilled: being of service. She was trying to get me to see how I could be of service.*
>
> *I remember feeling like a four-year-old, wanting to stomp my hands and feet and scream, "I don't want to be of service! I don't want to help people! I'm beaten down and jaded, and I don't want to help anyone!" I felt like crap about myself—what was wrong with me that I didn't want to help people? I thought I'd rather work with lab rats.*
>
> *I didn't know it at the time, but now I do—I see that dentistry is all about being of service to others, but that's the thing that burns us out. The thing that makes us feel so jaded is taking that concept too far.*
>
> *We sacrifice ourselves. We sacrifice our own wellbeing in the process of trying to be of service to other people, and that we actually push ourselves in the opposite direction until we deplete ourselves and can't do it anymore. And then we don't want to help anyone.*
>
> *That's something only a dentist would know.*
>
> –DR. LAURA BRENNER

The Best Conflict Avoidance is Conflict Prevention and Resolution

Many of us didn't learn conflict prevention or resolution. And, if we're associates or junior partners, we feel powerless to change entrenched conflict.

But conflict avoidance doesn't work. Conflict avoidance is actually conflict collection or conflict concentration. Those tensions will build until they explode. People-pleasing by avoiding conflict is like kicking a can of dynamite down the road.

How do we defuse that dynamite? Clear communication is the key.

We talk a lot about communication styles and phrases to use that will overcome resistance or defuse tension, but what makes communication work is its clarity, and clarity is rooted in courage.

It can be hard to tell the truth, especially for those of us who have an emotional stake in avoiding conflict. The truth may contain not only things like "That's not my job," or "I'm going to delegate this task/job to you," or, "That's not appropriate and can't happen again," but also "This is harming me, and I can't keep doing it." So long as we don't tell the truth, we can attribute tension or differences to poor communication rather than the real issues that we don't want to talk about. Those issues that you can't talk about are most likely the same issues that are burning you out.

The best way to avoid conflict is to prevent it or swiftly resolve it. Here are some steps you can take to resolve conflict in a way that will lead productively towards resolution instead of fueling drama and explosions.

STRATEGIES: Conflict Resolution

I had personal reasons to avoid conflict—my anxiety surrounding confrontation and letting people down—but there are practical reasons as well. When you're working in a practice you don't own, it can feel like your options are limited and that you must choose between bad or worse. I thought I had to choose between being silently, privately upset, or having everyone loudly and dramatically upset. It's not uncommon for people to pretend not to see the problems they don't feel equipped to solve.

I felt that "bad" would be having conflict, but "worse" would be acknowledging it and then having to do the work of dealing with it when I was already feeling emotionally exhausted and ill-equipped. There is a lot of practice management advice that is hard to apply when you're working in a practice you don't own. Happily, this conflict resolution process gives you a way to do what you can to improve things for yourself and others, wherever you work.

Talk with the other person. Trying to squeeze important conversations in between patients will mean one of you will be unfocused and distracted, which only leads to an unproductive meeting. Agree on a time and place to meet, where hopefully you won't be interrupted. If you are an associate and need to speak with the owner, plan a time at the end of the day. Also, make sure you both know the agenda. Communication and resolution are about sharing information, so be sure that your "we need to talk" is followed by agreeing on what you'll be talking about. And then make sure to stick to that.

Focus on behaviors and events, not personalities. Clarity and specificity are your friends here. Describe specific instances or events instead of generalizing about what you find dislikable about their personality, and speak about it in a depersonalized way. For instance, "When this happens…" will focus on the behavior, not the person, and therefore is more productive and useful than a phrase like, "When you do …" or "When you are …" When I was a new associate I didn't have this skill set. One time I brought the team's lack of respect for me to the owner's attention; it did no good. He didn't seem to care. In fact, he seemed to like the fact they respected him and not me. It stroked his ego. In hindsight, I should have said more. I should have discussed the issues in terms of office culture, but I learned from that experience about how to address conflict better.

Listen. It can be hard to listen, especially if they need to address something we've done wrong, or if we feel fear and defensiveness and listen to defend and deflect. It's vital that you listen without interrupting, with the intent to understand. When the other person finishes speaking, rephrase what they said to make sure you understood it, and if you didn't, ask questions to clarify your understanding. Basically, this is the assessment or diagnosis portion of conflict resolution, and the more clearly you understand the problems and the people, the more easily you can resolve the conflict. This was very hard for me to do at first. I was not good at taking criticism, and even now, it is uncomfortable. I'm better at it, but my first instinct is to get defensive, which isn't helpful or constructive.

Summarize points of agreement and disagreement. After summarizing, ask the other person if they agree with that assessment. If they do, then great, you can move forward. But if they don't, then you need to modify that assessment until both of you agree on the areas of conflict.

Prioritize the conflicts to resolve. Once you've both agreed on that assessment, then you can agree on which parts of the conflict are most important to you and your resolution. For example, request that the owner of the practice or staff prioritize making sure your schedule is full and productive. Then strategize to minimize cancellations or broken appointments.

Develop a plan together. Start with the most important and or most easily solved conflict, and agree on how you will solve it. Remember, plans always focus on the future. The important phrase that helps here is "Moving forward, let's…" It's productive and inclusive. For example, you could say, "Moving forward, let's have the front desk check my schedule a few days in advance and confirm all scheduled patients to keep my schedule productive and busy."

Follow through on the plan. While you develop a plan for resolution, remember that your plan, in order to be complete and actionable, needs to include future meetings where you'll continue these discussions. These discussions will help everyone feel heard and keep people accountable moving forward. To make sure, at the weekly check-in meeting, review if the plan was followed. Such as "My schedule still has holes in it or has cancellations. Can we work on fixing this?"

Keep discussing! It may take more than one discussion to resolve a conflict, especially if it's complex, long-standing, involves a lot of people or powerful personalities, or connected to how a practice is run. Conflicts don't spring up overnight and aren't always resolved overnight, either. Expect that this will take some time. Stick with these discussions—again, with agreed-upon times and places and agendas—until you've worked through each area of conflict. Maintain that collaborative, solution-focused attitude throughout. It's easy for the owner to fall behind on these meetings, which allows communication to slip. As an associate, you must make sure these meetings and check-ins are consistently happening.

Build on success. Bring in all the positive reinforcement you can. Look for opportunities to recognize progress out loud to the people involved. Respect and compliment other people's insights and achievements. Congratulate each other on any progress, no matter how small. For example, tell the front office: "Thank you so much for keeping my schedule full and productive and correcting the broken appointment issue."

If you can stay respectful, focused, brave, and positive, hopefully, these continued discussions will relax into ongoing, friendly communication that will begin to function as conflict prevention. Whenever there's a hint of *conflict with staff*, many dentists choose to ignore it. They tell themselves everyone involved is an adult who will be able to work things out on their own. Unfortunately, that isn't usually the case. Instead, negative feelings fester and lead to a tense work environment. Team members spend time gossiping and being negative, and that means they're less efficient and productive. If this gets bad enough, some employees look for a new job, which leads to more stress.[14] Not only is staff turnover costly, but it's also a culture killer.

You *can* improve your work life by changing how you work. Say yes to your own mental health and joy in the profession by saying "NO" to fear of conflict. Build a better balance by changing how you manage your own approach to conflict.

Many times as both an associate and an owner, I wish I had put more of these strategies into place. These strategies support my inner work and increase the health not only of my own career experience but also the culture in my practice. By learning them, I was prepared to handle the things I feared and moved from being frozen in anxiety to moving forward with increasing confidence.

---

[14] DentistryIQ. 2021. *Is one of these common problems causing stress in your dental practice?*. [online] Available at: <https://www.dentistryiq.com/practice-management/practice-management-tips/article/16367680/is-one-of-these-common-problems-causing-stress-in-your-dental-practice> [Accessed 28 February 2021].

Key Takeaways

- People-pleasing is a natural reaction to anxiety and being in a new situation.
- Associates may not control the office but can still set boundaries in their everyday work lives.
- Assess and address any issues you have with rejection and abandonment to decrease your anxiety.
- Transform your conflict avoidance into confidence by learning conflict resolution—then you won't be as afraid to speak up and say "NO."
- Don't set yourself on fire to keep someone else warm.

CHAPTER 4
ARE YOU A REAL IMPOSTER?

Do you fear being found out as a fraud?

Do you agonize over even the smallest mistakes or personal flaws?

Do you downplay your expertise, even when you are truly more skilled than others?

Do you attribute your success to luck or outside factors?

Do you react with sensitivity to even constructive or well-intentioned criticism?

Do you fear asking for help?

Do you feel like you aren't capable and don't belong?

You're not alone. Imposter syndrome is a very real thing that makes us feel like unhappy fakes.

Dentistry attracts many of the personality types who tend to experience imposter syndrome, and life in a practice creates many of the circumstances that trigger its manifestation. Entering a new role—for example, graduating or getting a new job—lights a fire of fear under us. It definitely did for me.

The Wake-Up Call

I had just graduated from dental school and was at my first job at a dental office in an area with a primarily non-English speaking Brazilian population.

I was just as bewildered as you'd expect, suddenly needing to earn my keep in the real dental world, with no idea how to interact with patients who spoke a different language or navigate systems to keep up with the volume. This opportunity had the added excitement—by which I mean stress—of an inability to communicate. Everyone at the practice spoke Portuguese except for me. Luckily the assistants could translate between the patient and me, but I'm not going to lie, there were a lot of hand gestures that resembled a bad game of charades.

I thought I had mastered the Portuguese word for "open your mouth," but every time I said it, everyone laughed, so I hadn't mastered it after all. On top of that, the office had an absentee owner on the days I worked. I was still finishing up my residency at B.U., so I was moonlighting there on Saturdays to earn some money and dip my toe in the world of private practice. I thought it would be a good thing that the owner wasn't there—no one to critique my work like in school, no one to compete with as far as getting patients in the chair, allowing me to do all the treatment planning and clinical work that I wanted to do. But, the lack of support turned out to be really hard. Being brand new to the real world of dentistry, it would have been nice to have a mentor there next to me to advise me and help me out if needed. Like on my third day there, a man in his early thirties walked in with pain in a non-restorable number thirty lower right molar. I thought: This will be an easy extraction, I'm going to make this guy's day and get him out of pain. He's going to walk home and say, "That was easy! Dr. Block was the best!"

Right?

Nope!

After about forty-five minutes of struggling with forceps and elevators, the coronal part of the tooth snapped off. The patient started breathing really quickly and started to hyperventilate.

The assistant said, "Doctor! He can't breathe! I immediately learned that I'm not good under pressure because I started yelling, "BREATHE! BREATHE!" over and over, thinking my frantic yelling was going to somehow calm him down.

When his panic attack didn't stop, we called 911. I paced like a caged tiger until the ambulance finally showed up. It felt like an eternity but was likely closer to five minutes. In came the paramedics to take him away, and because there was only one entrance, they had to roll him out on the stretcher through the waiting room full of patients. He hadn't been accompanied by anyone, so one of the assistants went with him in the ambulance.

Looking back, I find it humorous that after all that, I had to go into the waiting room and say, "Who's next?" The next patient put their magazine down, got up, and walked into the operatory like nothing had happened.

The story doesn't end here; it turned out the patient that went to the hospital didn't have any friends or family to call, so the paramedics brought him back to the practice. We had nowhere to put him, and at the ER, they had pumped him up with so much Valium he could barely stand up, so we put him in an open dental chair while he slept it off. While he was sleeping, I had a major wake-up call.

When I graduated, I thought I was invincible and could do any procedure on anyone. But this incident taught me how wrong I was. This was my *third* day of real-world dentistry! Like Dorothy realizing she isn't in Kansas, I realized I was no longer under the protective umbrella of school. There was no teacher to bail me out, and the practice's absentee owner was not a helpful mentor. I was in the real world now.

> *We have to make dentistry look entirely stress-free. It's all under control. No big deal. Nailed it every time. That's hard to do. It's very hard to do.*
>
> –ANONYMOUS

The Reality of Dentistry

My experience taught me three things about the reality of everyday dentistry:

1. Dentistry is hard on everyone involved

It's hard on the patient, and it's hard on us. Essentially, we are performing surgery on a moving target who is watching us work. They need the comfort our confidence provides and our skilled focus on the same small millimeter-sized space until we've treated their problem with painless and hopefully long-lasting work. We try to make this experience great for our patients, but sometimes dental work hurts, and sometimes it doesn't last as long as we hope, and the patient's expectations aren't met. It's normal for people to get upset and be afraid when they're in pain. Our confidence gives patients confidence, which reduces their anxiety and pain.

2. We compartmentalize to get the job done

The expectation is that we can easily struggle through the chaos in one room and then get up and move on to the patient in the next room like nothing happened, like we're fine. If we're not fine, we have to pretend even harder that we are. We compartmentalize our challenges and experiences. This challenges our mental health maintenance because this kind of sudden and repeated emotional transition without processing time feeds our anxiety, perfectionism, and people-pleasing tendencies, especially when we're still emotionally involved in the previous situation.

Showing confidence is the solution … and, eventually, the problem.

What happens when we don't feel that confidence? What happens when we need to perform this high-quality work in high-pressure situations not just once but all day? What happens when we can never admit we don't know something, ask for help, or have a bad day?

The kind of people who get into dentistry in the first place tend to share a lot of the same traits: competitive, detail-oriented, high-achievers who may naturally carry a lot of perfectionism and pessimism. These same traits can mix with how dental school and our profession work to create a situation where we keep feeling inadequate and alone.

Many new grads find themselves in a situation where they've graduated and need to start doing procedures in the real world, but it's nothing like it was in dental school. Like my experience at the Brazillian dental office, there are no teachers or classmates to help them out. They may be tackling procedures they're not very comfortable with while needing to make sure they look like they know what they're doing to the staff, the owners, and, above all, the patient. It's like the perfect fertilization for the poison ivy of imposter syndrome.

Lucky grads may be working for a really great owner who's willing to mentor and help out. But what about situations where the owner isn't there or is busy working and producing, or just plain doesn't want to help you out? You have to go in there, looking like you know what you're doing, and try your best.

As a result of the stress I felt early in my career, I tried to compensate by making my dentistry perfect. At the same time, I was also trying lots of new procedures and surgeries. Thoughts about my inadequacies tore up my stomach lining and kept me up at night.

We're often operating from a place of fear and belief—where we believe we need to both learn new things but also need to do everything perfectly. People who are feeling the crunch of imposter syndrome feel like they're not accomplished. They deny their successes and fear failure, but also fear success, too, because success can lead to even greater demands and higher expectations.

Many of us get stuck in a loop where the more we struggle, the more we need to look like we're not. Or, when we do experience some level of success, we can't enjoy it. In my second year out of school, I did one of my first full reconstruction esthetic cases. I started with the upper and lower front six. When I inserted the crowns, the patient was so happy. My assistant was happy, and there was so much positivity and joy in the room. Did I revel in this joy? Nope. I was so worried about not being able to finish the rest of the job that I couldn't join them in their joy. I said something like, "Well, this is a great start, but we have a lot of work to do!" I should have just been happy for the patient, but my fear of being exposed as a fraud overcame my joy. Getting caught up in imposter syndrome is an impossible cycle of expectations that cannot be met.

> *I'm currently working with an ER doc working in a high-volume metropolitan area. He cried copious amounts of tears. Life opens up to all the trauma; then he goes to the next cubicle, or the next crash cart, or the next patient, who's bleeding out from fifteen places.*

He's beginning to unravel all those stories that he mashes up like a trash compactor in order to move on to do the next thing. That compartmentalization creates tremendous isolation, which is the hardest place in the world from which to ask for help.

It's like, hey, it's a dumpster, but it's my dumpster, so I'm eating scraps and scared to get out of the dumpster and go out into the big wide world and ask for help, because what if it's worse?

That's what anxiety says: what if, what if, what if?

–PHIL HEARNDON MA, LPC-MHSP, NCC

What is Imposter Syndrome?

It's anxiety, depression, and a lack of genuine self-confidence.

It's feeling like you're a fraud or a phony and that everyone knows what's going on but you.

It's a certainty that what you're doing isn't good enough.

It's a belief that you are supposed to know everything and do everything but know nothing.

It's the isolation of never being able to struggle openly.

Imposter syndrome is a manifestation of anxiety that thrives in the same conditions that create burnout—isolation, stress, and a feeling of being overwhelmed. It's most commonly experienced as a young grad, associate, or new practice owner. And, I can speak from experience that it's true in all three instances.

For me, imposter syndrome showed up as anxiety, a reluctance to make myself vulnerable, a fear of conflict, and profound discomfort in my own skin. I needed to keep people happy so they wouldn't find out I wasn't the perfect dentist I wanted to be. I constantly had to hustle to achieve and to be enough. Achievement and people-pleasing were how I managed my anxiety.

Part of therapy is that there are three activities of the limbic brain, which is the emotional brain. One of them is limbic resonance.

Really smart people, moral people, tough people like you, and others in the profession are really good at smelling the room. Limbic resonance is that phenomenon where you walk into a room where no one's saying a word, and you go, "Oh, it's really tense in here." That's limbic resonance—picking up emotional smell.

Then there's limbic regulation. We were made to regulate off other human beings. Like, if a toddler falls back on her bottom, on a big thick diaper on a carpeted floor—he or she will look at their parents. If the parents freak out, the baby will cry. If the parents say, "Oh, you're okay, Baby," the baby will think, "Oh, I'm okay," and get up and walk on. That's limbic regulation.

If I walked into a room, and you had your head in your hands, and you were weeping, I would regulate off of you. I'd sit down next to you and go, "Eric, man, you okay? What's going on here?" I wouldn't go in and go, "Hey man, can I tell you this joke I heard? It's hilarious." I wouldn't do that because I'm regulating off of you.

So when we're in people-pleasing, we can read the room through the goggles of fear of abandonment. Then as I regulate off of people, I might make up stories about their facial expression, their tonal inflection, and all through the goggles of "I'm going to be abandoned here. I'll do anything I have to do, not to do that."

And that third area of limbic activity is called limbic revision. In limbic revision, I begin to see through different goggles. I begin to take care of myself because therapy has revised my limbic brain. Abandonment is not my story. I'm looking through different lenses now.

ARE YOU A REAL IMPOSTER?

That's what great therapy does.
—PHIL HERNDON MA, LPC-MHSP, NCC

My anxiety started in dental school. My instructor pulled me aside and said, "We've got a problem here. We need to get on the same page about whether you're going to graduate."

He was right to worry—dental school didn't come easily to me. I was a B- student in high school, and it took me until my junior year of college to learn how to study, and it wasn't until Tulane that the fear of not having career options made me turn the jets on and get straight As my last year and a half. My teacher's warning put a fire under me—the fear of failing. I had to fight hard for every grade in my undergrad and dental school.

I graduated from dental school at twenty-seven years old, but I looked fifteen—and, honestly, I felt fifteen, too. The gap between what I needed to do to graduate and what life in a practice entailed left me totally unsure of myself. After I graduated from Nova Southeastern College of Dental Medicine, I knew I wasn't clinically ready (nor was I even close to being emotionally mature enough) to go into private practice. So I went to B.U. for a two-year implant residency. I was in a situation where I had to fit expectations and look like I knew what I was doing. Even though I'd worked very hard to graduate and wasn't a fraud, I still felt like I was, compared to the more senior dentists around me. Even at the age of twenty-nine, I looked like I was eighteen. I can't tell you how many times I heard: "You look too young to be a dentist" or, "You look like you're my son's age."

As an associate right out of school, I felt a lot of imposter syndrome when I needed to present treatment to patients who'd seen a senior dentist for twenty years, and now I had to win them over while being a fresh, nervous grad who looked like a kid. It was especially difficult to try to present to patients who had very different lives than I did—sixty-year-old CEOs, scientists, professors, people with money. I felt like a fraud, knowing I was proposing treatment to people with millions of dollars and a boat while I was living with roommates and trying to pay off my dental school loans.

I'd get nervous, lose confidence in my assessment skills, second-guess myself, and sometimes I would actually end up talking the patient out of treatment.

A study in Medical Education of 477 dental, nursing, and pharmacy students found that 27.5 percent were experiencing psychiatric levels of distress closely associated with perfectionism. [15]

How Imposter Syndrome Leads To Burnout

I remember one time as an associate where I was doing a surgical extraction. I felt overwhelmed, but I tried to pretend I had the confidence even though I didn't feel it. This particular patient was an executive-type that was in his early seventies and always showed up in a suit and tie. The plan was for me to do an extraction of his lower right premolar and immediately place an implant. Easy peasy, right? I did everything wrong. I was impatient and rushed into the extraction and tried to muscle it out. Then I heard the old familiar noise of a root snapping. CRACK, AHH SHIT!!!! I spent about sixty minutes unsuccessfully trying to dig the root tip out and ended up referring him to the oral surgeon. I ended up losing the case, the patient, and a lot of sleep. I remember telling

---

[15] DentistryIQ. 2021. *How real dentists conquer real stress.* [online] Available at: <https://www.dentistryiq.com/practice-management/practice-management-tips/article/16367701/how-real-dentists-conquer-real-stress> [Accessed 28 February 2021].

the assistant things like, "Find this bur," or "Get those forceps." But, on the inside, what I was really saying to myself was, "What the hell am I doing here? Where's my teacher? I don't know what to do!"

On the outside, I needed to look cool, calm, in control. I felt like a duck on a smooth pond. On the surface, I tried to glide gracefully, but underneath the hidden water, my feet were paddling like crazy. So, I faked it. I faked it all with the best of intentions. I knew that patients in the chair are often pretty anxious themselves and that as the dentist caring for a patient, I needed to be the calm one in the room, even though with all my anxiety, I wasn't. It was the only way I knew how to keep up with the realities of everyday dentistry.

I didn't let on to patients or the team that I was stressed. I put on a happy face and tried to please everyone. I'd make sure I was "on" with each patient, bringing energy and positivity to each person like they were my first and only patient for the day. I'm an introvert, and pretending to be extroverted like this for hours a day, out of fear, was utterly exhausting. I needed downtime alone to recharge, but the job needed me to be someone else, so that's what I forced myself to do. Not only did I want to make my patients happy, but I also wanted to make ALL my staff, coworkers, and patients happy. This was a cumulative disaster.

Because I needed to inhabit a dentist persona that didn't really reflect me, I wasn't great at anticipating which patients weren't a good fit and would end up with difficult patients that I'd keep trying to please with increasingly worse results. I took on procedures that were outside my comfort zone because I felt like I needed to keep proving myself. To make matters worse, because I was saying yes to everyone, the staff and other dentists would send me all the kids and phobic patients. For me, these were the most difficult patients, but I was too introverted to say no. I also wanted to be busy and make money. So I said yes. They took so much energy I'd internally say to myself: "Whatever I just made on that procedure was not worth it." Then, once I was feeling nice and burned out, I'd shove all my feelings down and compartmentalize my pain and fear while moving onto the next patient in the next chair and start the process all over again. I would work to get through the day, to get through the week to the weekend, work to get through a few months until I could go on vacation.

The refusal to seek help is an unfortunate cultural attitude in dentistry that is perpetuated and nurtured on message boards, at seminars, during study club meetings, and at conferences. People believe that seeking help is admitting failure.[16] I know I did! That's why I didn't do it.

Treating my patients and then doing hygiene checks for eight hours a day with no breaks utterly exhausted me. I felt like I had two choices: I could make sure I was always "on," keeping everyone else happy all day, and then go home and collapse—or I could choose to be openly unhappy and have all the same exhaustion plus the tired anxiety that would result from knowing so many people were mad at me.

So, based on this perspective, I made a tradeoff and decided that instead of making everyone unhappy, I'd keep all the unhappiness contained in myself. But this trade-off only works if you're only working with great, compliant, motivated patients and well-trained staff.

People-pleasing and poor boundaries are a package deal; if you feel like an imposter and unworthy to be where you are, then why

---

[16] DentistryIQ. 2021. *How real dentists conquer real stress*. [online] Available at: <https://www.dentistryiq.com/practice-management/practice-management-tips/article/16367701/how-real-dentists-conquer-real-stress> [Accessed 28 February 2021].

would you deserve the respect that boundaries represent? If your needs don't matter, why would you rock the boat to meet them?

This elevated expectation for emotional and professional performance sent my happiness and well-being plummeting as my anxiety soared. My stress and isolation had burned me out.

One thing I am passionate about doing as a dentist and as someone who has personally benefited from therapy is to normalize and destigmatize our need for help and support.

> *I think there should be dentist support groups. Support groups where you don't go on Facebook and see that everyone's doing perfect stuff because I get a lot of x-rays in my office that don't look perfect. I don't know who perfect dentists are, but their patients aren't coming to my office very frequently. Just having people be more honest would help us all feel less alone—I think we have very little honesty out in the open. Finding people that you can be honest with about your work and surrounding yourself with those people instead of the Facebook people who are, you know, the dentist down the road or I don't know. There's just so much pressure, and we're so isolated.*
>
> –ANONYMOUS

Who has Imposter Syndrome?

Imposter syndrome correlates with mental health issues but isn't recognized as a psychiatric disorder. It's more of an occupational one. It's brought about by the same issues that affect job satisfaction and burnout—if you're really high-achieving and worried about details and perfection, you're likely to suffer from imposter syndrome.

There are several things that increase the risk of developing imposter syndrome, including:

High expectations. When a person grows up in a high-achieving family, they may internalize feelings of inadequacy that become unreasonable expectations. Likewise, people who grew up easily achieving a lot, like gifted kids, may not know how to cope when faced with increasingly difficult tasks.

New situations and challenges. When a person experiences a recent change in circumstances or opportunities, like graduating or getting a promotion, they may feel like it's undeserved or that they're inadequate for the new role.

Marginalization. While anyone can develop imposter syndrome, it's especially common among ethnic minority groups.[17]

Common comorbidities. People who develop imposter syndrome often already experience depression, anxiety, or perfectionism or may have undiagnosed learning disabilities like ADHD or dyslexia

Professional culture. People whose professions include both isolation and a need for an image of competency are especially at risk, partly because they are afraid of the consequences of asking for help.

> *There are plenty of resources out there, and currently, they're remote, which is ideal from a time-management standpoint. So take advantage of that. Figure your stuff out now because you can't be helpful to a patient if you have internal chaos going on, and you're not your best self.*

---

[17] Bravata, MD, MS, D., Watts, MA, S., Keefer, Ph.D., A., Madhusudhan, MPH, D., Taylor, Ph.D., K., Clark, BA, D., Nelson, PsyD, R., Cokley, Ph.D., K. and Hagg, Ph.D., H., 2019. *Prevalence, Predictors, and Treatment of Impostor Syndrome: a Systematic Review.* [online] ncbi.nlm.nih.gov. Available at: <https://www.ncbi.nlm.nih.gov/pmc/articles/PMC7174434/> [Accessed 28 February 2021].

> *You cannot practice with conviction in the face of people who are traditionally anxious seeing you in the first place. You have to be your best self, the rock. You have to be the captain to your clients and make them feel like you will help them get through what they will probably perceive as a stressful, anxiety-provoking visit with you.*
>
> *You know, it's not like people view going to the dentist like they view going to Disney World. So the assumption should be that your patients need a lot of reassurance and handholding. You can't do that if you don't have your stuff together.*
>
> –DR. ALDEN CASS

Imposter Syndrome: Solutions

When I graduated from Nova Southeastern, the same instructor who'd warned me I wasn't doing well pulled me aside again and said, "Hey, this is like a minor miracle here!"

I told him that I was headed to an implant residency. He was impressed and said, "Well, if you can do this, you can do anything. You'll just have to work at it." I'm really glad to be where I am now, and it has taken a lot of work—something that I know other dentists know a lot about. We've all had to work hard to get to where we are now.

But even now, twenty years later, those same thoughts I had as a dental school student or as an associate can come creeping back. The voices in my head would say: "Hey Blocky, who do you think you are writing a book? You avoided any class in school that involved a paper or essay like the plague!"

Here's what I do when that happens:

I accept my limitations

I've accepted the fact that I'm really good at not being good at something right away, and that's ok.

It takes me a lot of effort to develop skills, more effort than it apparently takes my peers. There were some classmates I had in dental school who did things so quickly and effortlessly that they made it look easy. You know the ones I'm talking about! One of my classmates, Ernesto, got all As in his science classes and clinical work while I worked hard for my Bs and Cs.

I've accepted this about myself, and I do what it takes to learn and do things my way. I know it'll take me ten times longer to complete certain tasks. Just ask my wife how long it takes me to build our kids' toys. If the box says "ten minutes," I multiply that by a factor of ten, and, yup, those toys will be done an hour and a half later.

I now expect this kind of learning curve, and when I learn new skills, I work within that curve, taking the time I need to apply new knowledge to myself. I watch YouTube videos, I observe other people using the skill or completing the procedure, and then I practice over and over until I eventually master that skill.

I now know that polishing my clinical skills will always mean taking the time to watch more experienced dentists work and then giving myself time to try and fail. I went through a million burs when I was figuring out how to do crown prep and fillings, or as I tried the matrix band and wedge on and off a hundred times. It doesn't mean I'm bad at dentistry—it means I'm great at knowing how to learn.

Now I say NO to some procedures in order to say YES to myself and my career

I struggled for a long time with endodontics and surgical extractions and dreaded seeing them on my schedule every day. I wanted to love my job and enjoy it, and after a lot of trying, I finally decided that these procedures just weren't in the cards and that they simply made me too stressed. I said "yes" to my long-term career and myself by saying "no" to those procedures and the draining sense of dread that followed in their wake. I now refer these procedures to my associate or an outside specialist, and I feel great about it. Blocky Bucks!

You may find that some procedures or aspects of our profession just aren't for you. That's great! If you know that something is hard for you, accept it. Work realistically with it. If you don't accept where you are and work around things, you may keep comparing yourself to an impossible standard and falling short of where you could be if you worked within your strengths. If we tried to help the patient in our chair with the abilities we had, we did what we could. And maybe doing what we could means accepting our limitations and referring out. Hey, either way, we're making sure they're getting the care they need, and that's our job.

Imposter syndrome can't thrive where people are being real. You don't have to be great at everything to be a good dentist. Identifying those things you don't love to do or aren't great at and letting go means you're succeeding at prioritizing your health and the longevity of your career. I'm not naive to the fact that this is a lot harder for a young dentist or associate with massive loans, bills to pay, and the pressure to keep a full schedule, but you can't do it your whole career without becoming resentful or leaving the profession altogether. Constantly working on patients or procedures that you don't enjoy will catch up to you. The stress is cumulative. Ask me how I know.

I set goals based on realistic expectations

Perfectionism feeds imposter syndrome by forever moving the goalposts. It's great to reach outside our comfort zone so we can keep growing, but if some part of us inside refuses to recognize our accomplishments, we can end up in a loop where we're giving it our all while convinced we're doing nothing worthwhile. That's a terrible place to be, mentally, emotionally, and professionally.

Dentistry is an inexact science that can lead to a long line of disappointments. Sometimes things don't turn out the way we hoped they would, despite the effort and skill we've expended. A plus B doesn't always equal C. Like NFL kickers, hockey and soccer goalies, or ninth inning closing pitchers, I don't get too high with the highs or low with the lows. Temper your personal expectations with the knowledge of the things you can control and the things you can't.

Those of us with perfectionism can hear a message in the phrase: *"Did you do your best?"* that isn't intended. Part of perfectionism and pessimism is that we persistently ignore how we succeed and focus on failures that are normal human failures or only feel like failures in comparison to an unachievable ideal.

Setting goals is a way to anchor those goalposts so that we can see our own progress despite disappointment and prove how much we've accomplished, even if we don't feel that way. Be a good friend to yourself and replace "Did you do your best?" with "Did you do what you could? Were you honest with yourself and your patient?" Will you have to redo that procedure for that patient at no charge in the future? Maybe? Don't beat yourself up over it.

Business leaders recommend setting SMART goals, goals that are specific, measurable, attainable, relevant, and time-bound. A SMART goal focuses your efforts, where a dumb goal leaves you flailing, unable to achieve perfection. So, for instance, a dumb goal would be, "I want my practice culture to be better." It's relevant, but it's also vague, unmeasurable, and doesn't have an end date. Instead, try, "I want to reduce turnover by 20 percent in the next year." With a SMART goal, you have a deadline, you can measure and set benchmarks, and you have a focus so you can come up with a plan. I believe in writing down your goals or saying them out loud often, don't let them just live in your head.

Use your goals to define what you can do. If you set goals, you can see when you achieve them; the goalposts don't move.

I cheer for myself

One of the patterns that leads to imposter syndrome is not calibrating or celebrating accomplishments. Disrupt perfectionism! Believe in yourself! Start now! Now I would jump up and down for that patient who was so happy for her new anterior crowns. I would take part in her joy, and instead of dreading the next step of her treatment, I would look forward to the future happiness I know I can provide her. I would bring the staff, assistants, and other dentists in to feel her joy and celebrate the win. You stopped that goal kick, closed out the ninth inning, or kicked that extra point. It's ok to celebrate the wins, so you don't drown in the losses.

When I started my website www.DealsforDentists.com during the Coronavirus quarantine, I kicked doubt's ass by writing on a whiteboard a huge YOU CAN DO THIS! Whenever that fear crept up, I'd look at that. I also wrote down other daily and weekly goals and would look at them every day. I did the same thing when writing this book, and I do the same thing in dentistry. I believe in myself, and I ignore the negative doubts and beliefs that tell me I can't succeed or that my success isn't real.

Do whatever it takes to remind yourself that you are here for yourself. Kick doubt's ass! You can do it!

I go old-school for peer support

My mom and both of my sisters are writers and editors. When I felt nervous about writing this book, I'd reach out for support from them, and I could feel it coming through. When I feel nervous about my dental career, I reach out to other dentists for support.

Dental school is full of stress, but the undeniably great thing about it is the high level of peer connection and support. At Nova Southeastern, I had ninety-nine other classmate peers to commiserate with every day. They were right there next to me day in and day out. Peer engagement was so accessible that I took it for granted. But then we graduate, and we lose that connection with classmates and mentors and the chance to share stories and bounce ideas off each other and have the feeling of being around people who know exactly what you're going through.

I can't say I don't compare myself to other dentists, but I can say that if I do, I know it's not really going to help. Comparison isolates us. Cooperation and community are what bring us together. We're all struggling with our own stuff, and we're not really in competition with each other anyway. There are nine other dentists in my little town of only 25,000 people, and unfortunately, I don't know most of them. In reality, once the patient is in our chair and is a patient of record, other dentists are not the competition; our real competition is whatever problems or expectations are keeping our patients from getting in the chair or paying the bill. Our real enemy is our isolation. We should all be in this together. We all live these parallel lives like parallel universes. I suggest getting to know the local dentists in your area. The more you know your local colleagues, the more you can work as a team, and there is less chance someone will throw you under the bus. Start a study club or Facebook group for the local dentists in your area to engage.

Recreate the best part of dental school by connecting with other dentists. Connecting with another dentist is still my favorite way to learn anything, whether it's a procedure or a new perspective. Think of it as an extension of school; we're working together on our How To Be Happy Dentists degree.

We all need friends and mentors. Recovering even 1 percent of the camaraderie we felt in school can be hugely helpful for getting through tough times, especially early in a career. There's nothing like getting off the phone with a former classmate or colleague after swapping stories from the dental trenches—it's like its own little therapy session. I had a good dentist friend that graduated with me from B.U. He and I would talk at least once a week. It was so refreshing to swap stories about patients and treatment and just engage about life after dental school. I would get off the phone, and I felt like I'd just had a therapy session. It felt so good to know that someone else was going through the same issues that I was. We got each other because we were both going through the same experiences. Tragically he died in an avalanche in Canada over ten years ago. I really miss him and the conversations we could have. I think of him often and hope his family is doing well. Nobody can understand what you are going through quite like another dentist.

Having a mentor, who's nice, who's there, who's a kind person and wants to help you was so valuable.

–ANONYMOUS

Sometimes people do need that connection to other people who are also not doing well, who are going through the same hurdles and stresses, and it helps to hear how they're running their business and what pitfalls they've gone through. It's always helpful to hear that in times of crisis.

–DR. ALDEN CASS

Types of Imposter Syndromes and Strategies

Just as there are many different risk factors for developing imposter syndrome, there are many different manifestations of imposter syndrome. Researchers have nicknamed each of these manifestations: Soloists, Experts, Natural Geniuses, Superheroes, and Perfectionists.

People may be predominantly one type, two types, or a combination of all of them at once. Each type of imposter syndrome has its own precipitating factors and recovery strategies.

Let's talk about the different forms imposter syndrome may take and additional strategies for addressing each one.

Soloists are individuals who like to work alone. Asking for help or accepting it feels like broadcasting weakness or incompetence. Their productivity is the source of their self-worth. Interdependence can feel heavily transactional.

Strategy: It's hard to perceive everything about ourselves by ourselves accurately; we each benefit from outside perspectives to see what we're missing. Shame keeps many people from confessing their feelings and needs. It takes strength and courage to break through the shame that can keep people suffering alone in silence. Good therapists, mentors, and coaches work to help us to see our innate worth and root our self-regard in a foundation of who we are instead of what we do. You deserve nothing less.

Reassert your rights as a human being, and change your internal script from "I should be able to always complete everything alone" to "Everyone has the right to be wrong," "Everyone has the right to need help," and "Everyone has the right to have a bad day." Then put your rights into practice by enlarging your comfort zone. Start small by asking coworkers for small, mostly inconsequential things, and work your way up to relying on others for assistance.

Experts never feel satisfied with their level of understanding and consistently underrate their own expertise even though they are actually highly skilled. They often feel like they don't know enough and are always trying to learn more.

Strategy: Diligence is great, but frequent and pervasive self-doubt and dismissal are like constantly being attacked in your own head. Many people with anxiety and self-doubt feel stupid even when it isn't warranted. Separate your feelings from facts—having a feeling of being stupid is very different from enacting an objective experience of being stupid.

If you're one of the only people in your field of view who looks or sounds like you, it's natural to feel like you don't fit in and don't have real expertise. For instance, if you're older or younger, from another community or culture, especially one underrepresented in your profession, it can be all too easy to come across doubt from others that you may then internalize. Instead of taking your self-doubt as a sign of your ineptitude, recognize it for what it is: a normal response to social stereotypes about competence, intelligence, and belonging.

Experts may benefit from connecting with a mentor or a trusted peer with whom they feel safe and who can help replace the Expert's feeling of never being enough with a more reasonable standard of knowledge and ability. Practice saying "thank you" to compliments like when a patient says: "Wow, that wasn't so bad!" Connect with those who are truly supportive because a sense of belonging fosters confidence. Break the cycle of self-invalidation by very deliberately patting yourself on the back. Praising yourself, especially in front of others, can feel very strange at first, but it'll get easier as you practice it.

Natural Geniuses have impossibly high expectations for their own performance and achievements and are crushed when they don't quickly succeed.

Strategy: Natural Geniuses can benefit from a healthier response to failure by addressing their belief that not only must they do things perfectly, but they also need to do perfectly in a fast and easy way. Remember that you do not have to be the smartest person in the room in order to be worthy or likable, and that everyone who starts new things feels uncomfortable in the beginning.

Check-in with peers on how hard everyone has to work and how normal initial failure tends to be. Try not to fall back into comparison and competition; each person has their own strengths and weaknesses. I used to go to a lot of symposiums and lectures where the presenter would show amazing cases with cutting-edge research to back them. I'd walk out of the lecture impressed but also intimidated, feeling down about my own practice or skills. As if I was doing substandard work compared to theirs. I wish these lecturers would show their failures and mistakes—like how many cases did not turn out perfectly. If you are going to show me a perfect ten case, also show me some ones or twos. We've all got them, and we need to normalize the process.

Change internal scripts from "I am only successful if I succeed easily and immediately" to "Keep moving—I'll get this next time," "Learning takes time," and "The only failure is not to try." Pat yourself on the back every time you do try. Reward yourself extra when you fail because failure is an opportunity to begin again better each time.

Superheroes feel inadequate and push themselves to work as much and as hard as possible.

Strategy: Superheroes will benefit from having help seeing and appreciating their own strengths and innate worth so that they don't have to lapse into workaholism as a replacement for belonging. Connect with people inside dentistry, so they can share their experiences and help you recalibrate your work/life balance. You may also benefit from connecting with people totally outside dentistry who value you for non-work-related reasons so that you don't feel the pressure to perform for them in order to have worth.

If you, like many other superheroes, often picture impending disaster and experience work-related stress, as a result, do what professional athletes do. Visualize successfully presenting to a patient, completing a procedure, or calmly talking to your team. Each time you feel that anxiety rising, with thoughts about your inadequacy, picture yourself calmly winning, and at the end of each visualization, tell yourself what a great job you did.

Talk to therapists, mentors, or coaches who are familiar with the challenges and standards of dentistry, and get help with drawing clear boundaries on how you can spend your time and energy at work and away from work. The benefit of trusted help like this is that when you cannot trust your own estimation of yourself and what is a reasonable expectation for performance, you can trust someone else's. Chances are they are going to be a lot nicer to you than you have been. You are enough and don't have to earn the right to adequate rest and basic respect.

Perfectionists are never satisfied with their work and feel it could always be better, and that it isn't only because of failure on the Perfectionist's part. They fixate on flaws, real or imagined, and often forget their strengths. Perfectionism is often rooted in anxiety.

Strategy: It's great to care deeply about your work and strive for excellence, but to do so at the expense of your mental health is to make work the enemy of your health and happiness. Mistakes are inevitable, and the truth is that you cannot be 100 percent perfect, 100 percent of the time. All-or-nothing thinking robs us and our days of recognizing things and people who are imperfect yet good.

Pick the one thing that will be your priority in a given moment, and try not to let routine tasks be that priority. That's exhausting and the fast lane to burnout. Change your ideal from doing everything perfectly to doing most things comfortably. Acknowledge that circumstances will have an effect on you and that 80 percent is still good enough, and forgive yourself for the inevitable mistakes. Being perfect is not required to be good. And it's a great idea to get support from a therapist, coach, or mentor as you begin to make life inside and outside your head a kinder and gentler place.

> *Clearly, there are things from your childhood that you learned from watching your parents as you grew up, but a lot of this stuff I'm dealing with—fear of failure, lack of confidence—that comes from self-esteem, which is built up through obstacles you've overcome in your life.*
>
> *And the more you have to face early on, the more you overcome, the more resilient you become in the face of setbacks as you get older. The more and the more you overcome it, the more resilient you are in the face of setbacks as you get older.*
>
> –DR. ALDEN CASS

Summary

- Imposter syndrome can affect anyone but especially those with perfectionism, anxiety, or depression; minorities or anyone underrepresented in their field; or those who've recently had a major life change.

- There are several subtypes of imposter syndrome; you may be one, two, or all of them.
- Imposter syndrome is exhausting and contributes to burnout.
- Get help from a therapist, mentor, or coach to address your fears that lead to imposter syndrome and reset your expectations from impossibly high to reasonable and attainable.
- Reach out for support from peers whom you trust and can be yourself with.

CHAPTER 5

HOW TO HANDLE REJECTION AND CONNECT WITH PATIENTS

After you graduate from dental school, life comes at you fast.

Dental school dentistry and real-life dentistry are wildly different. When I was a student, I remember that we'd talk over the patient like they weren't even there and that I could take my time. My first implant placement at B.U. took me three hours! THREE HOURS!!!

Then I entered the real world of dentistry, where I had to keep learning difficult procedures on the job, perform them quickly, and on difficult patients. I thought I had to take on every case and every patient, no matter how difficult, and I gave it my all. I had imposter syndrome and wanted to do everything really well, and every rejection felt like a personal failure.

I worried about patients rejecting my treatment plans or my best efforts to treat, and I dreaded rejection and dissatisfaction that could lead to bad reviews or, worse, to being sued. I was stuck in a terrible downward spiral.

I was so anxious about that impending disaster that my fear tore up my stomach and kept me up at night and led me to retreat from procedures I'd previously been comfortable doing. Then I'd take on another difficult patient, feel crushed by more rejection, and the spiral would tighten.

Dentistry, by its nature, exposes us to a lot of rejection. It just comes with the job, and the worse rejection feels, the more quickly this job will burn you out. I had a huge fear of rejection when I started out.

The most common reasons why we engage in these patterns are fear of rejection, fear of abandonment, and a misunderstanding of what we're responsible for and therefore must control. These reasons lead many to people-pleasing behaviors that, over time, create patterns that rely on poor communication and lack of boundaries. These patterns affect us, our teams, and our patients.

> *Toxic shame is a phrase that says I should be all things to all people. And if I'm not, I'm inadequate, I'm no good, and I'm frustrated and lay awake at night.*
>
> *What if I end up saying yes when I need to say no? What if I say yes to things I need to refer out? Fear of not being enough—inadequacy, feeling defective—that toxic shame button gets activated.*
>
> *It's scary at first, but so much more freeing just to say some things I can do and some things I don't need to do. Those I'll refer. There are going to be some patients that I think I'd be great with, but they're not going to go with treatment for whatever reason. If I can hold those ideas integrated into my story, then that's a heck of a lot better.*
>
> –PHIL HERNDON MA, LPC-MHSP, NCC

Do You Fear Rejection?

Everyone experiences the fear of rejection at some point. Some of us have life experiences marked by painful rejection, and it makes sense that our brains will keep us afraid of anything that may risk our safety. But even those without traumatic events may find themselves increasingly frozen by fear of rejection.

It's a vulnerable thing to admit we are afraid of this; we relabel it as caution or distance. Ironically, our fear of rejection may even lead us to fear admitting to our fear!

Fear of rejection will keep us from great opportunities, from life-giving connections with others, and from reaching our potential as dentists and humans.

Here's how fear of rejection may be manifesting in your life:

You wear a mask

Fear of rejection leads us to put on a public face that disguises our truth. We plaster on fake smiles and try to make other people happy, worried that people will reject us if they know what we're really like and who we really are.

This mask keeps us from forming the relationships in our professional and personal life that we badly need to support us. Reaching out for connection and support is a key part of blocking burnout.

You try to please everyone

You agree to do things you don't want to do—you take on things that make you uncomfortable or that ask too much of you. And it works—temporarily. Inevitably, people-pleasing leads to so much exhaustion that you begin to lose sight of your values and reject your own life that you've worked so hard to build.

You turn down new opportunities

Fear keeps you safe from danger; chronic anxiety redefines everything as a danger, including the things that help us grow. If you find yourself seeing everything as too risky, including reaching out for help or having a better work/life balance, then chances are your fear of rejection is burning you out.

You don't speak up or share your real thoughts

If you don't share your opinion, ask for what you want and need, or stand up for yourself, then you're probably operating from a place of fear of rejection. This fear can lead to an unclear communication style, where you try to protect yourself by using language that makes you sound disconnected and safe from things that really matter to you. For example, if you really needed a staff member to call a patient but smothered your real intentions with phrases like, "If you'd like to do that, that'd be okay," that's passive-aggressive communication. There were many times, as an associate, I didn't speak up. In one office, I would go in and check the schedule and see that I had one patient while the owner's schedule was double-booked. Instead of addressing it directly, I'd ask him how he was doing. He'd say: "I'm so busy, buddy." It felt like he was rubbing in how busy and successful he was while I sat there twiddling my thumbs. I should have been frank with him about it, but instead, I internalized my anger.

You resent others

When it feels very risky and difficult to openly and clearly ask for our needs to be met, then it's not hard to follow that to its logical conclusion, that those who force you into having to face the

HOW TO HANDLE REJECTION AND CONNECT WITH PATIENTS

discomfort of speaking clearly are doing you harm, and that you're entitled to have people read your mind.

We do this because we figure that rejection won't hurt as much when it's not spoken aloud or faced directly. So we act out of fear, and hint, give back-handed compliments, manipulate, or complain, all rather than just directly addressing our concerns to the people involved. This way of interacting with others will inevitably build to all the conflict we've been trying to avoid.

> *A person who is dealing with—or, rather, not dealing with— unresolved abandonment, rejection, or humiliation will struggle.*
>
> *For instance, a patient not booking an appointment? That's rejection.*
>
> *Emotionally speaking, rejection and abandonment are synonymous with death. A child's limbic system says, if they utterly reject or abandon me, I'm not viable by myself.*
>
> *Your big old dentist's brain knows that's not literally true. Your literal life doesn't depend on that patient coming in, but limbically and emotionally speaking, it will reach back into those territories of terror. When someone rejects you, the brain says, I'm not viable. That's the emotional impact.*
>
> *So when you do have that limbic revision through the therapeutic process, you're able to say, I issue an invitation. I gave what I needed to give to the patient for information. And if they say no, I can deal with it knowing I brought my craft to it. Yes, I can feel sad they didn't say yes, but I can move forward with the same passion I had before.*
>
> –PHIL HERNDON MA, LPC-MHSP, NCC

How To Handle Rejection

Fear of rejection fuels the fires that lead to burnout. Stop fueling that fire by addressing the fear at its source.

Accept rejection as part of the job. There is no way to rejection-proof yourself. Your recommendations will be rejected many times over the course of your career. Expect it and plan for it by accepting that it's painful for you and that you deserve to plan to support yourself through that.

It's not about you. It's tempting to give in to our perfectionism and try to outwork or out-achieve rejection, but it still wouldn't work because it's not always about you and your skills. There are so many reasons why a patient will reject a treatment plan—because they lack money, motivation, or an understanding of their need for treatment.

Let them own it, and let it go. Something I tell myself and my staff is that we should never care more about a patient's mouth than they do.

Redefine success and failure. Patients have a whole multitude of reasons why they reject treatment. The only failure here is to stop trying. If you did your best to assess and present, then you succeeded. What happens after that is up to the patient.

It's an opportunity in disguise. It's hard to hear no, and it can be even harder to hear why. Take a deep breath and see this as feedback on things you can work on in your practice, whether it's educating patients on dental health, creating payment options, or support with managing insurance. Once you've had enough practice dealing with rejection, you gain the ability to make the criticism constructive. I used to feel hurt when a patient wouldn't rebook with me or if there was a note in the chart that said they didn't want to see me, or they only wanted to see my partner. But now I understand that not everyone is going to like me, and it's not personal. Sometimes it's just not a good fit, and it's better for everyone to accept that up front.

Create a process for responding to bad reviews. I used to be terrified of bad reviews, but telling myself that they wouldn't happen wasn't realistic. What was realistic was coming up with a process I could count on to help me. That transformed the prospect of a bad review from a crisis into just another manageable event.

Once you've done the work to address and manage your own fears, you'll be ready to make great changes in how you interact with others, which will go a long way towards rebuilding health and safety in your job. As a bonus, when we aren't operating from fear, we take off our masks and are free to have authentic connections with our patients. And patient connections are key to running a great business.

How to Connect With Patients

It took me 10,000 clinical hours to not only develop my clinical skills but also develop my verbal and interpersonal skills. My conversations with patients and answers to their questions are much less exhausting now. I take control of the room and conversation. It's like a time-managed stage production. I know I have a few minutes to chit-chat, and then I need to get that patient numb, so we don't get behind in the schedule.

Whether it's talking about clinical dentistry or about each other's lives, my time management and emotional energy isn't as exhausting as it used to be. My patient interactions, for the most part, are much less stressful.

But it took years to hone these skills. I'm more polished in how I present and sell treatment. Even better, when I talk to patients and staff, instead of worrying the whole time what they're thinking about me or what a fraud I am, I'm on a nice and relaxed autopilot. I know the keywords to say and how to respond to certain questions.

Here are the strategies I wish I'd learned earlier in my career:

Build your expectations with boundaries. Being 100 percent focused on making your patient happy (and your coworkers happy, too) sounds great on paper, but it's a nightmare for your long-term professional satisfaction. The patient certainly matters, but you matter, too. Disentangle from the need for their approval. This will lower the stakes in conversations and make you far more comfortable and willing to connect. A good therapist or life coach can help you see where your boundaries need work and how to improve them. There are many excellent books about setting boundaries in professional settings—I recommend *The Practice RX* by Dr. Dino Watt and *It's Okay To Be The Boss* by Bruce Tulgan.

Hone your interpersonal skills. We learned clinical skills in school, not interpersonal ones, but dentistry is very much a people-centered business. You'll likely enjoy your job more if you equip yourself with more practice in communication. Get the help you need to learn to read the room and respond in a way that doesn't exhaust you.

There are many excellent books, videos, and online resources about how to connect with people. Ask a coach, a friend, or a staff member with great connection skills to help you. Find a course, search for videos on YouTube, or connect with other dentists online with Dentaltown, or follow The Stress-Free Dentist on Facebook and Instagram for tips about how to connect with patients.

One of the best ways I've found to connect with people is to find something positive that we have in common. This has become a lot easier since I married and started a family—I ask how their kids are doing, and they ask about mine. Asking people about themselves is a great way to show that you're invested in them and that you care. For example, if the patient is an engineer, I'll chat about my intraoral scanner or CT scan and digital implant workflow. If they're a scientist, I'll talk about new dental materials. If they're into marketing or sales, I'll talk about how we market at the dental office.

You don't need to become a different person. I'm still very much the introvert I was when I entered dental school. But practicing interpersonal skills will leave you less frustrated and exhausted by patient and staff interaction and also will help your natural intentions come through more clearly.

Pace yourself. Don't sacrifice your emotional well-being for someone else, especially not on a regular basis. I have several patients that I know will need a great deal of emotional energy. Some are phobic and cry; some need lots of hand-holding and warm, fuzzy encouragement.

I can handle these patients in small doses, but I know the high energy expenditure these patients require would burn me out if I had to do it on a daily basis. Make sure your scheduled appointments are allowing for a good balance.

Don't care more about someone's mouth than they do. We've all been there. We got the x-rays, found the problem, made the treatment plan, and … the patient refuses to go through with it.

It's easy to get frustrated and discouraged by this. We've trained so hard to help others; it's upsetting when they won't participate in their own care. It's painful to experience rejection. This frustration and discouragement, when repeated, will burn us out and may make us dread working.

Yes, be passionate and diligent and provide a great patient experience that answers all their questions and educates them on the risks and benefits of the procedure you offer—but don't beat yourself up if they don't move forward. Let the patient's compliance be their decision, and their unwillingness to move forward be their problem. Remember that you did what you could and move on. Also, remember that a "no" now does not mean a "no" forever. Often, patients need time to process, and or their problem needs to get worse before they are ready to say yes.

So often, we are the ones creating the hard and fast rejection that we forget the patient might just need more time. Let them know you understand, and you will check in with them next time. A "no" is often just a "not yet."

Avoid hot topics. Some dentists may enjoy discussing these topics, but I certainly don't. I don't care what patients do on their own time; whoever is respectful to my staff and to me is welcome in my office. But, I personally avoid talking about politics, religion, and money. These topics come with a lot of emotional energy attached, and I'm interested in conserving that energy for my own enjoyment.

I prefer to find common ground that my patients and I can connect over. Develop a repertoire of these topics, and practice keeping the conversation positive. You'll develop a feel for this as you keep practicing patient connection.

The topics I find that work best are the ones that make people feel happy: Their family, hobbies, trips, work accomplishments, things they're looking forward to. Once I got married and started a family, I had a lot more in common with my patients and found that rapport was easier to build because we could connect through family-related topics.

Figure out your comfort level. I'm at a place now where I'm comfortable with both my clinical and communication skills, and I feel fine about working on friends and family. Some of them want to see only me. Some feel too awkward and will see anyone but me.

I always tell my friends and family that it's up to them whether they want me to work on them and that if they want to see my partner or associate, that I'm happy they're making the comfortable choice for them. I don't take offense.

HOW TO HANDLE REJECTION AND CONNECT WITH PATIENTS

Some dentists don't want to work on people they know or on their staff. Each dentist needs to figure out their own comfort level regarding working on people they know. Respect your comfort levels; the more comfortable your work is, the more likely it is you'll enjoy it. Let go of expectations for discomfort. Respect yourself and your inner happiness and mental energy.

> *Over time, I've become a bit better at saying no to patients. "I can't do that." "No, it's not happening." "You can go somewhere else if you want that done."*
>
> *But—we had a patient maybe eight months ago (obviously, I'm still thinking about it), and he was one of those who refused to get x-rays.*
>
> *I should have just said, "I don't think we're the right practice for you." It just wasn't worth it. He had a bad attitude, and I knew I didn't want to be near him and that I wasn't going to be looking forward to him being in the office.*
>
> *So why didn't I just tell him so he could leave? Instead, I'm trying to win him over.*
>
> –ANONYMOUS

Red Flag Patients

Just the other day I was dealing with a difficult patient. He was trying to dominate the room and the conversation and dictate the treatment. He kept contradicting me and talking over me, insisting that he didn't need a crown and he didn't like x-rays. He cut me off in the middle of my presentation and started telling me how he wanted the treatment to continue. As my eyes glazed over, all I could see was a red flag.

Of course, not every patient falls neatly into the "easy patient" or "red flag" categories. Patients come from a variety of backgrounds and bring with them a complex spectrum of dental histories, personalities, and financial circumstances.

When I say red flag, I am not talking about the patients with phobias or financial issues. I'm talking about the ones other people call PITAs (Pain in the asses).

Red flag patients are exhausting and take up a lot of mental resources. This is the 90/10 rule of patient management—10 percent of the patients take 90 percent of the energy. Their treatments are straightforward, and things are fine. But then there is that small segment of patients that take far more energy, whether because their case is deeply complex and incompatible with what our practice can offer for treatment, or—as in this patient's case—because they're hard to be around and deeply resistant to giving up control.

I used to try to negotiate with red flag patients, but experience has shown me that this is a really poor investment of time and energy. I wish I'd known sooner the vital importance of selecting only cases that are a good fit, both in terms of my emotional health but also in terms of creating success in clinical applications and patient interaction. As I've accumulated time in practice, I can sniff out the potential red flag patients, and I'm sure you have that ability too. What we need to get better at is cutting ties and letting these patients know we aren't a good fit for their needs. Associates, tell the owner and the staff if you don't feel comfortable working on certain patients or doing certain procedures. You have to speak up. If you don't, you'll get these patients all the time because the owner doesn't want to see them. Be clear if you are hesitant to treat, and have clear communication about it.

Managing Difficult Patients

Catch them early. If you can, screen the red flag patients out early before they come into the office. Ideally, you'll get your practice to the point where you and your staff can find the red flag patients early and often, through initial phone calls, if possible. Usually, red flag patients can be noted in their issues with assessment, treatment, payments, or they speak poorly of their previous dentist.

What does their body language say? Here's one way I can tell if someone is likely a red flag patient: if, when you enter the room, they're standing or sitting perpendicular to the chair with their feet on the floor. This statement in body language says that the patient has control issues or trust issues and tells me that maybe I should, too.

X-rays and exams are great for diagnosing all kinds of problems. Another red flag I've found is whether a patient will consent to a doctor's exam or an x-ray. It's too hard to try to persuade reluctant patients or work around this by making exceptions. I now have a firm policy that I won't work on a tooth that hasn't been x-rayed within a reasonable period of time and that all new patients need a full series of x-rays and/or panoramics. If you have a solid x-ray policy in place, that right there will select out people who will not cooperate with treatment.

There are some patients who've had medical treatments involving a lot of radiation or who have a fear of radiation exposure. If they are willing to work with me and promise x-rays in increments with the understanding that I cannot fully diagnose without x-rays, then I will work with them.

Train your staff. Policy-based boundaries are only as good as the staff's enforcement. It's crucial that you get your staff on board with this; if you find they're not x-raying patients, you need to resolve that issue with that staff member.

I find that what helps with staff training is if I ensure they fully understand this policy and the reasons for it. My failure to diagnose is a major liability, and accuracy in diagnosis is crucial for successful treatment. Patients can refuse treatment but not diagnoses. That's totally unacceptable and not worth your time and energy.

Catch and release. Patients who won't participate in assessments are likely to reject treatment plans and are likely to refuse to pay. It's easy to feel like time is money and that having spent an entire thirty-minute consultation with a patient invests you in a continuing professional relationship. It doesn't. Let them go. It's not worth it. Catch the signs of non-compliance early, and let them move on.

I find the best way to encourage this is to have the front desk tell the patient that we have no history of x-rays and need them in a given dollar amount. Often, they cancel future appointments and good riddance. The same goes for patients that are unhappy and are requesting a refund for treatment. To me, I would rather give them their money back and defuse the situation rather than potentially irritate the patient to write a bad review. It's not worth the "Blocky Bucks."

Support your staff. Your staff will likely be more willing and able to catch and release red flag patients early and often when they know that they have your support and that you will ensure that they do not have to tolerate misbehavior. Nothing says "red flag" like someone who's giving your staff a hard time. Fill your office with patients that respect your policies. They are the ones more likely to move forward with the treatment that you recommend. Non-compliant or diagnosis-denying patients are exhausting and unproductive. They aren't worth your or your staff's valuable time or mental energy.

Now that I've worked on changing how I manage my emotional experience of dentistry, I'm enjoying work again. I balance my focus equally between patients and myself, whereas before, I would sacrifice anything to try to make things work with patients and staff. And now that I practice careful case selection, the people I'm presenting to and treating are as a whole far nicer than before. I used to ask the front, "Did they schedule?" and was crushed when they didn't. Now I don't take that as a personal rejection. I know that I'm confident in my skills, treatment planning, and educating patients with all of the options, risks, alternatives and that if they didn't book, it's not because of me. I've reconnected with my love for my job, and you can, too.

Key Takeaways

- It's normal to fear rejection. Figure out the root of your fear and take it seriously.
- Case selection is your friend. Learn how to spot red flag patients, and refer out patients who are not a good fit.
- Find whatever help you need with learning communication skills. Read books, connect with peers, find mentors, work with a coach.
- Don't care more about someone's mouth (or job!) than they do.
- Bad reviews are a fact of life. Build a process, trust it's there, and let go of the fear.

CHAPTER 6

OFFICE CULTURE — IS YOURS TOXIC?

After I graduated, I found myself in a totally new set of circumstances. I didn't have to study anymore, and I was finally going to make some money, which seemed great, but then I realized that I needed to improve my clinical skills and, terrifyingly, use them on real patients in real-time. Suddenly I didn't have a teacher to rely on who was looking over my shoulder, guiding my work. Instead, I had a boss I needed to satisfy. I didn't have to deal with clinical requirements or board exams or the bureaucracy of the school environment, but I had a volume of patient care to keep up with on a schedule. Gone were my fellow students; now I had staff to please, owners to impress, and patients to treat, all while using unfamiliar equipment according to someone else's workflow. And, of course, I had a massive debt load that I was bringing along behind me.

I had an outer culture I was dealing with: what the owners wanted, what the patients needed, and the personalities of the staff. I had an inner culture, too. My imposter syndrome made me deeply uncomfortable in my own skin, and that impacted my ability to communicate or set boundaries. My people-pleasing was both a symptom and a source of the increasingly toxic inner and outer work cultures that were quickly burning me out. In the face of all the demands, I figured that if I could just make everybody happy, then maybe things would be ok.

But they weren't ok.

> *About a year into my third job, I saw that my boss, who was nearing retirement age, wouldn't retire. He had initially started taking Mondays off, so I could have all the patients on Mondays. Then he started coming back in again on Mondays.*
>
> *I also dealt with really difficult staff that were family members and not held accountable. Day-to-day, I carried the weight of the world on my shoulders and just didn't have any support.*
>
> *So I was like, I've tried every kind of practice, and I'm outta here, you know? If this doesn't work out, I'm done.*
>
> –DR. LAURA BRENNER

Are Things Ok at Work?

Office culture is a fact of business life. You can either lead the office or let the office lead you. You can choose to create your own culture from the ground up, or you can choose to stick with the culture you've been handed. The right culture makes your practice profitable and interesting; the wrong one drives good people away.

Because nobody teaches us how to run a business, and because all the moving parts are overwhelming, many of us just take whatever culture comes with the office. Many people purchase a practice only to find that they've also bought a poor office culture—or they retained a team that worked well before but who can't handle the new personality mix. Even one toxic employee can affect the rest of the team.

OFFICE CULTURE — IS YOURS TOXIC?

Earlier in my career, the office hired a new assistant who'd only been on the job for two weeks. She showed up to the practice that morning hungover with glassy eyes, smelling strongly of alcohol; I assume she'd gone out and partied the night before.

The other assistant and I somehow got through the morning with her. When we reached our lunch break, she climbed into a dental chair to take a nap. The other assistant and I left for lunch, hoping that when we got back, we could wake her up and complete the second half of the work day. This was fine, right?

Wrong. She was in such a deep, heavy sleep that the other assistant and I couldn't wake her up. We tried for a while and then gave up and moved our instruments to the other end of the office and worked without her while she loudly snored away.

Luckily, it was a Saturday, so we had the rest of the office to ourselves. We could hear her snoring all the way down at the other end of the office. Looking back on it, she probably had a major case of obstructive sleep apnea. #You-cant-make-this-stuff-up. It could have been worse—but it should have been better.

Can you imagine how it would affect a patient to be worked on by an intoxicated employee, or how it looks for there to be an employee sleeping it off while others work? I couldn't accept her behavior and choices and run an effective practice. Since I was the associate, I felt like I had to say "ok" to her behavior. But doing that was also a surrender of my own expectations of professionalism. I cared more about being a "nice guy" and not making waves than about my office culture, and it hurt me, my team, and my patients.

Maybe, like me, you've accepted things and have told yourself this is just how dentistry is in the real world. But it doesn't have to be. You don't have to say "yes" to that behavior or culture.

It's not always obvious when things aren't okay, and that's especially true if we've had a pattern of not holding people accountable for their choices. This story is funny, but it also shows the impact of one team member's behavior in affecting the work culture around them.

One common factor in burnout is unsafe or unsupportive coworkers or working conditions. Some practices may have that one employee that stresses everyone out; some offices have a culture where everyone is participating in patterns that keep stress and drama high.

Are you feeling driven away from your work? Do you dread going to the office? If you do, is it possible your staff dreads coming to work, too? How do your patients experience your office environment?

Let's assess the support/stress ratio in your work culture.

Office Culture Health Assessment

Assessing your current work environment starts with you. You need to be honest with yourself. Look in the mirror and ask honestly if the poor culture is because of you. The culture starts from the top. Ask your team too. Their input here is valuable.

1. Do you feel emotionally and physically safe at work—with colleagues, with the tools and equipment provided in this environment?
2. Do you understand what the practice expects of you and how to do it?
3. Do you feel safe sharing my ideas and trying new things at work
4. When you make a mistake, are you corrected in a respectful manner, and are you clear on how to improve?
5. Do you receive acknowledgment and feel appreciated at work?

6. Can you trust team members and colleagues to support you as you work together to make your practice succeed?
7. Do you feel you matter to both your team and your leaders?
8. Do you feel your leader supports your career development?
9. Do you feel motivated by your practice's mission, vision, values, and leadership?
10. Would you invite a friend to work here?

If your practice culture could be better, why is it still bad? A big reason is that most people can't stand change. They'll hang onto something that barely functions just because it's less scary than taking a chance on something that could actually be good.

A great way to help yourself or a team prepare for possible needed changes is to invite your/their authentic experiences and insight. Those answers can help point towards which changes need to be made in which order of priority.

Still not sure? Let's talk about what a toxic culture looks and feels like.

Symptoms of Toxic Work Culture

Unsafe or morally questionable working situations

It's emotionally exhausting to constantly have to worry about your well-being, both physically and mentally. When this condition persists, it selects for team members who don't care about safety or morality.

Unrealistic workloads or deadlines

Feeling overworked and under-supported is a fast track to burn-out. Even when short-term goals call for requiring your team to stay in overdrive, that kind of adrenaline doesn't encourage people's best teamwork or health.

Workaholic behavior

If it's considered normal in your practice to put work before everything else and work to the exclusion of health, then burnout becomes part of the work culture.

Excessive absenteeism, illness, or fatigue

Just as increasing physical pain and illness is a sign of burnout in an individual, it can also be a sign of burnout in a team.

Constant conflict

Conflict is stressful, and not everybody has constructive ways of dealing with it. We'll talk about that more later as we cover communication and boundaries.

Strained or absent interactions between team members, or teams and leaders

Sometimes conflict feels so overwhelming that people would rather turn a blind eye and stop communicating altogether in order to avoid problems they don't know how to solve.

Aggressive bullying behavior

Whether from leaders to the team or between team members, bullying creates a hostile environment that affects everyone.

Gossiping and exclusion

Drama undermines the good we try to do in our work. It's hard to communicate

Favoritism

Indulging in double standards and discrimination is a sure way to lose a team's trust and can create an official flowchart of authority and then an unofficial one. This kind of disparity makes it hard to solve problems and improve as a team.

Poor communication and unclear expectations

This is a common factor in conflict and burnout. How can people do well if nobody has defined "well"? How can people work together as a team when their roles are unclear?

A managerial style that excludes, ignores, or contradicts employee feedback

People love a leader but hate a dictator. Customizing leadership to address team concerns is what makes a team your team.

Wage gaps

Any gaps due to any criteria unrelated to job demands and performance—e.g., gender, ethnicity—will have an impact on both your current staff and on future staff.

Causes of Toxic Work Culture

Culture is the collection of beliefs that support, inform, and justify behavior; culture is formed by choice. Choosing not to address culture is a choice; refusing to take action is a choice, so culture is a choice. Whether consciously chosen or unconsciously permitted, here are the beliefs that people maintain that can support a culture that is unsafe or toxic.

Discriminatory Beliefs

Unchallenged bias can lead to imbalanced work policies or unequal compensation.

Dehumanizing Employees

Treating people as assets or things instead of as people will lead to poor policies. Assuming employees are lazy, greedy, and/or expendable adversaries will inevitably create a poor working environment.

Information Guarding

Some people take "information is power" to heart and keep back information, which leads to poor communication and unclear expectations.

Aggressive or Hostile Leadership

This style of leadership leads to resentment and fear and ultimately undermines leaders who engage in it.

Lack of Accountability

Whether a leader or team member, everyone needs to be accountable. Accountability is a basic part of fairness, organization, and safety.

Lack of Appreciation for Good Work

If effort goes unrecognized, it's not hard to see why some people stop making an effort.

> *The reason that the owner hated me is because when I was pregnant, her father made a couple of inappropriate comments to me and also touched my stomach.*
>
> *I told our office manager. All I really wanted was for it never to happen again, but she kind of just shrugged it off. It was an awkward situation: How am I supposed to tell my boss that I'm uncomfortable? The office manager didn't handle it well. She was horrible. She wasn't paying attention and didn't care. She was chronically overwhelmed and didn't seem to like her job and didn't seem empowered in the position to do anything.*
>
> *When someone comes to you and tells you that they were uncomfortable with someone touching their stomach—if you have an office manager who can't see that, you need to be paying attention to it. Even if just to say, "That's horrible; I'm so sorry that happened."*
>
> *So I wrote a letter and had it added to my file there. I'm a very by-the-book person, and I'm not gonna not say something when something's wrong. I wanted this to be formal, like, you guys need to pay attention to the fact that it's happened, and it can't happen again because I can't work here and be harassed*

for being pregnant. Then they brought in a lawyer. I think that's probably what set the owner off.

I think that practice was just growing so fast that they couldn't quite keep it all together. And there were things that hadn't been dealt with, and they didn't want someone around who was pointing them out. I spoke up about sexual harassment, and I think that might've led to my termination. I think I was too dangerous of an employee to have around, you know? Like this person is going to cause some problems, let's get rid of her before that happens. I think it was a combination of that, and they didn't exactly have a place for me.

I definitely think they treated me differently because I'm a woman—a hundred percent. There are things that people say to me that no one would ever say to a man. For harassment and for trauma, my residency was the worst. I wouldn't recommend that place or the culture.

–ANONYMOUS

Why do we stay in toxic work cultures?

It seems counterintuitive that anyone would knowingly stay in a toxic situation, but those of us who've struggled in our career while feeling the pressure to professionally or financially keep up probably already understand how dentistry's complex demands create the outer and inner pressure that make situations go from bad to worse.

That's how many of us have found ourselves working in a situation that doesn't bring out the best in us or others. Some of us have had experiences as associates trying to get by, maybe dealing with owners or staff who have their own way of doing things that we disagree with. Maybe other dentists in toxic situations have recently transitioned into owners and are overwhelmed by the additional personal, logistical, and financial responsibilities that come with managing a practice.

We may also be familiar with the patterns of justification and denial that help us persuade each other and ourselves that it's not that bad, that it's not a big deal, that it's ignorable, that it's how all practices are. We do this to avoid the conflict of recognizing poor behavior and holding bad actors accountable. I worked in a few offices where new staff members were treated poorly because they were new to the club. The click of legacy staff made new team members feel like outcasts. Unfortunately, this behavior was tolerated and made for poor culture.

It's common to feel like we can't change patterns, especially if it appears that many other people are invested in maintaining a painful status quo. But we must change them in order to stop burnout at its source. You deserve a better experience, and so do the people around you, whether it's your colleagues, your team, or your patients.

It's vital to create solutions that include clearer communication, better management, and more supportive systems and workflows, and we will talk about those here and in the following chapter. The best solutions are built on accurate diagnosis.

Cleaning up Culture: Solutions
Assess the situation

We begin by first understanding how we got here. Knowing what led the problems to develop and what led us to burn out in the first place is what helps us to create the solutions that will help us to heal and grow and prevent the same burnout from happening again.

Connect and get some feedback

If you're hurting at work, chances are you're not the only one. Connection with others is a major part of emotional health. Honest, open feedback is absolutely crucial for leadership. Asking others to share what their experience is at work honestly is a really helpful way to get additional perspective on what can be a subtle and complex problem.

Take accountability

The above advice is doubled if you're in leadership at your work. A healthy practice is one where communication goes both ways. It's essential that you have a way for your staff to share their concerns safely. If you're not sure how to make this shift, start with an anonymous comment box. This lets people share honestly about real issues without fear of immediate retribution and is a step towards rebuilding lines of communication and trust.

A note to owners with new associates: Treat them well. New grads and young associates are looking to you for mentorship and support. They want to perform well for you, so help them do it. Outline your expectations of them clearly and encourage them to take ownership of the parts of the practice where they will thrive. It will benefit you in the long run with less turnover, happier patients, and a healthier practice overall.

If you are an associate who is working in a toxic environment, take accountability for yourself and get out. If the situation won't change, you change your situation.

Bring in an expert

Everyone has biases, no matter how hard they try to stay neutral. If you are still struggling to unpack your office's issues, bring in an expert to identify the problems and resolve the conflicts. This is especially important in a practice that's struggled for a long time and where trust has eroded too much to repair on your own. There are plenty of great coaches and consultants out there. They've seen it all before, and getting help allows you to focus more on your job.

Make new rules, and hold everyone to them

This is key to taking power away from bullies and halting the spread of toxicity. When you stop letting things slide, no matter how small, you will encourage and retain the kind of diligent people every practice relies on for success—and you'll weed out the people who aren't willing to work in a healthy and accountable way.

Set reasonable expectations for how fast this will change

Change is uncomfortable, and a lot of people don't want to do it. There's a reason why people burn out before changing, and it's because change is stressful! It's easier to paper over the real problems with superficial management or system fixes rather than to the deep work of confronting why we permit or engage in behaviors that harm us and others. Repairing a toxic culture begins with naming that we have one.

But if there's anything burnout teaches us, it's that we have to name the fears that motivate us so that we can address those fears and begin to transform our inner landscape into something that will support a transformed outer landscape. The best way to resolve these issues in our offices is to resolve them in ourselves.

Key Takeaways

- Toxic work cultures increase the anxiety that leads to people-pleasing and accelerates burnout.
- Toxic work culture is marked by a lack of honesty, communication, and accountability.
- You can either keep a toxic culture or keep good employees, but not both.
- Owners and leaders must act to increase accountability and communication.
- Associates may not control the office but can still set boundaries in their everyday work lives.

CHAPTER 7

DON'T LET THE MONEY BURN YOU

Don't let the numbers do a number on you.

> *I moved out to Denver and got a job in a really fast-paced private practice. The owner took over 150 different insurances, and I would see about thirty patients a day. I was really excited if I had a procedure that was new! I'd call my mentor and ask, can you walk me through this. And he'd tell me how to do it over the phone. I wasn't scared—I was excited and hopeful. I was excited to have a paycheck and not have to study for tests anymore. I thought my future was going to be a lot of fun.*
>
> *Then, about three years in, that just ... slipped away. Some experiences in the office came back to bite me in the butt, and that made me jaded and scared. I feared getting sued. I'd go home and worry. I felt like I needed all my work to be perfect, and I didn't want my patients to get mad at me.*
>
> *It created a ton of stress. I started to question what I was doing in this career. Could I hack it?*
>
> —DR. LAURA BRENNER

Dentistry, at its best, can pay really well, but we take on a lot of financial risks to get to that point. And where there's risk, there's stress.

Dental school focuses only on clinical skills, but our success as dentists has as much to do with our business savvy as our chairside skills. Most of us end up needing to learn about practice management on the go while we're doing our best to help patients and survive our student loans. And, of course, managing our mental health while we're at it.

> *I thought, "I hate this. I need to quit." That was in 2004, and because of the economy at the time, I convinced myself that it was a bad time to do that, that I should feel lucky just to have a job.*
>
> –DR. LAURA BRENNER

There's a lot of stress involved in money and dentistry, whether it's the massive debt load with which we start our career, the stress of trying to learn how to get up to speed in clinical work, the risk-benefit calculations of transitioning to an owner, or all the numbers management and fiduciary responsibility that comes with managing a thriving practice.

Let's talk about several things that dentists find stressful about money and strategies you can use to manage both the systems and the stress.

Being an Associate

> *The downside was how fast I had to go as a new grad. I was trying to do the procedure and make money off of it, and you just can't make money that fast. It was hard for me; it*

was hard for my employer. There are always some frustrations when you're an associate.

—ANONYMOUS

Money raises the stakes. Most of us don't know the real numbers and personal costs of dentistry in the real world until we get there, and by then, we're already deeply in debt.

There were so many times in the first part of my career where if I could've left dentistry, I would've. I imagined getting a job where I could sit in a cubicle and go all day without talking to anyone, a job where I wouldn't have to worry about getting sued constantly. I contemplated going back to school to study law, reasoning if I was a lawyer with a DMD, then I could be the one that held the power and do the suing. But I needed to make dentistry work, partly because of money. I graduated from dental school and implant residency with $300,000 of debt.

The only way to work ourselves out of debt is to be very productive and generate revenue clinically, and that can be challenging when we're still growing in our clinical skills, not to mention the need to work faster to meet the volume needs of a busy practice.

This means that our best-case scenario as an associate is that we have to work fast and hard and find ways to learn a lot on the job in order to make financial headway. But associates have the added challenge of working hard in a practice that isn't theirs. As junior staff, associates may not have the authority to address issues in office culture because they are not in control. Associates don't have the resources to make the systemic changes that would support better physical and mental health for themselves and the team. They're at the mercy of the practice owner's whims.

This difficult situation is a perfect storm of burnout risk factors—the associate experiences unclear expectations, physical and emotional exhaustion, and lack of support.

In that middle job, the boss offered me a percentage of collections with no guaranteed minimum on his part. I thought, "I'll crush that." At the previous office, that boss had offered me a percentage of production, and I always doubled my base salary, so I went into this naively thinking that it would be the same. And it was a big mistake.

I share this for people looking to get into different associateships. I learned that it's good for me to be paid on production because that puts me on the hook, but it's good for the owner to be accountable in some way, too—otherwise, he could just take everything he wanted, if he wanted to.

–ANONYMOUS

Strategies for Associates

When there's so much going on, it's tempting to sacrifice your well-being for your career.

Don't. You cannot afford to ignore the toll this kind of unsupportive environment takes. Now is the time to address your emotional health and put boundaries in place to protect it while engaging strategies to meet your everyday needs.

Be as picky as possible

Find a practice where you can communicate well with the owner and trust them. Unclear expectations lead to working too hard on things that aren't your job. You need to avoid this by finding an owner who can be consistently clear about their expectations. Ask me how I know. I stayed in some associateships way too long. If your chair isn't staying full, or your owner doesn't treat you well, it's time to move on.

Find a mentor

Trust me, I know it's hard. When you first get out of school and get your state license to practice dentistry and start making some real money, most of the time, you just want a job. You don't have time to wait and find that perfect associateship. You only have so long before you need to start paying those loans back. Ideally, you'll be able to find a practice where the owner will mentor you and directly support your growth. If not, take the opportunity to observe the owner performing procedures whenever you can. Also, ask the owner questions during your interview. Ask about mentorship, and get references from past associates.

Feeling like an imposter or like you don't have the competence you need can contribute to fatigue that leads to burnout. Know that it's okay to be a beginner, and then work in a reasonable, self-caring way on advancing your skills.

Reach out through online communities to find other dentists who are just a step ahead of you in career development. Watch procedures on YouTube or learn on Dentaltown.com. Make the best of the internet by connecting with resources.

Build Boundaries Now

Because associates are managing so much debt and are the new kids in the practice, it's easy to slip into habits of people-pleasing. Our work should be patient-centered, but please remember that sacrificing your inner well-being in order to please others is a great way to end a promising career. If you intend to be in this for the highly remunerative long haul, then you need to invest now in the boundaries that will allow you to continue working without wearing out prematurely.

If you find yourself resenting patients or dreading dealing with them, that's a solid indication that it's time to step back and redraw the line between what is yours to carry and what is theirs.

Know Your Numbers

If you're an associate, make sure you're getting paid properly. Check your day sheets. All too often, procedures are billed under the owner's name, and you need to address that immediately. There is nothing more frustrating than finding out that someone else got paid for your procedure. I learned this the hard way when I discovered that someone I worked for as an associate had not paid me anything. I ended up having to take them to small claims court.

The bottom line is this: you work hard, and you should get compensated for your work.

> *Looking back, this is kind of an interesting thing that I don't really talk about that much. With associateships, there's that divide right between owners and associates. I think owners feel like they've worked so hard to get where they are and that associates take that for granted. I see associates on the other side, feel like, hey, I'm here. I could make your life so much easier. You can pay me to do the work for you.*
>
> *In [my] second associate job, I had come from a job where patients were handed to me, and I liked that. I wanted that, but there was this expectation that I should be building the practice as well, but I just didn't know how to, and I really didn't want to. I think a lot of associates feel that. We just want to do the dentistry, and I understand how that's frustrating for owners. But as associates, that's hard too.*
>
> —ANONYMOUS

Ownership

Transitioning to ownership is another huge financial and emotional event in a dentist's life.

We may not have paid off the debt we incurred starting our career, and buying a practice or building one from the ground up can send our debt from the hundreds of thousands into the millions.

One of the greatest benefits of ownership is being able to run the practice however we want. It's great to organize a whole office around our own desired specialties and our desired office culture, including the supports that help us maintain our best emotional and physical health.

> *I can have a pretty good living as a three-day-a-week associate at a busy practice.*
>
> *That's another hard thing. I've really changed my expectations of income from what I thought ten years ago. That's what bothers me to this day—this is not where I intended this career to take me. But maybe there's some benefit to putting that aspect aside a little bit and accepting I'm just on a different path.*
>
> *You're an owner; I've got lots of friends who own their practices. They're doing very well. And it's like, I'm frustrated that I'm not in that pool, but at the same time, at this point, I can't worry about that too much. I am what I am, and having that bigger role and that expected income—what would be the point if I couldn't do it?*
>
> *So, it still bothers me to think I'm not where I thought I was going to be and may not ever go there, but I have to accept it. It's always on my mind. It's always in the back of my head.*
>
> –ANONYMOUS

If you have a goal to own your own practice, be sure you know what you're getting into. If you're becoming an owner to have a better work-life balance, it's possible you can meet that need better as an associate in a great practice. Being an owner requires oversight and management of absolutely everything—finances, business management, vendors, and resupply.

As an owner, it's your job to pay all the bills and keep the lights on. It can be stressful to manage people, especially if you don't have experience or great boundaries. Being responsible for the financial well-being of several employees is a weight of responsibility that isn't right for everyone.

I don't want to discourage you from practice ownership. Buying or building a practice is a great way to take your career and income to the next level, and for many of us, owning our own place is the fulfillment of the dream that led us to dental school in the first place.

> *I got the call after Christmas that it didn't end up being AML leukemia. They told me that initially. I went once again to Google, and I think that, at my age, from what I remember, there was about a 30 percent chance of being alive in five years. So that was a very eye-opening experience.*
>
> *I had to leave that very day to go to Nashville and start treatment at Sarah Cannon Cancer Center. Then I dealt with several days of wrestling with this idea that I might not be around for my kids and do I have all my ducks in a row for if I am gone.*
>
> *Then when I finally saw the actual treating doctor, you know, he came in, and he said, "Well, we've sub-typed it. You've got AML leukemia. It's a very rare type. It used to be the deadliest form. But now we've now figured out a treatment regimen that is 90 percent effective, but you're in a low-risk*

category, so, in all likelihood, after chemo, you're going to be totally fine."

So, it was just this up and down, all this stuff. That was a huge relief, obviously, at least wondering if I was going to live through this.

But I still had all these other concerns. What am I going to do to keep my practice alive? And, you know, disability doesn't kick in for three months, what am I going to do in that time? Is this going to kill my teaching and all that stuff?

I couldn't leave my hospital floor because I had no immune system at that point. It was like being in COVID before COVID, you know? Masks everywhere. Everyone couldn't talk to me unless they had a mask and all this stuff.

But my sister visited with a mask, and she asked me, "What are you going to do with your practice? How are you going to make ends meet?"

And I just remember saying, "I don't know. It's probably going to go under."

–DR. CORY GLENN

If you're thinking about buying a practice, here are some things to consider:

Get real with yourself about what you can handle

Not every personal situation is conducive to supporting taking the step to ownership. If you or a loved one has health challenges like cancer or chronic pain, you may need greater schedule flexibility and fewer on-the-job responsibilities in order to maintain your work-life balance.

Check the numbers

Do the research on what to look for so you know how to recognize a financially healthy practice. I'm not going to pretend to be an expert but you should find someone who specializes in helping dentists purchase a practice. Don't try to do all of this yourself. Get the right help. Buying a dental office will most likely be the biggest decision of your life and you want to make the most informed decision you can. I'll just give you a snapshot of this process. Here are some of the things you need to plan on doing before jumping into ownership:

- Check tax returns.
- Create a cash flow model.
- Look at lease agreements.
- Evaluate employee lists, including salaries and benefits.
- Above all, find expert help in the things you're unsure about.

Embezzlement

Embezzlement is a major issue in our industry. Susan Gunn, a national speaker and certified fraud examiner, told embezzlement course attendees at the 2011 Chicago Midwinter Meeting that three out of five professional practices are being embezzled. After the meeting, Gunn stated that approximately 80 percent of course attendees either suspect embezzlement in their practices or they recently had been victims of embezzlement.[18]

---

[18] Stapley, DMD, K., 2011. *No one is totally immune from theft, embezzlement.* [online] Dental Economics. Available at: <https://www.dentaleconomics.com/practice/article/16394651/no-one-is-totally-immune-from-theft-embezzlement> [Accessed 28 February 2021]

Like all negative events that involve people and money, this is a problem with two parts—the emotional side, and the practical side. Both parts of the problem need solutions.

It's self-evident that embezzlement costs us financially, and that's best minimized through changing our practices and systems. That requires changes to our work routine that we may resist. The key to overcoming that resistance and protecting ourselves against embezzlement is to address the emotional side of the issue.

This experience convinced me of how embezzlement is both financially and emotionally costly, and that it's cheaper and less stressful in the long run for owners to change their daily experience by knowing the numbers.

The Emotional Costs of Embezzlement

Emotionally speaking, embezzlement is a betrayal, and betrayal is something that shakes our core, because it can lead us to stressful self-doubt—if we trusted someone who financially harmed us and our team, then how can we trust ourselves in the future?

Many of us hate to talk about embezzlement because we may feel shame about having been taken advantage of by a trusted employee. It makes us feel vulnerable, and like we've failed as owners. It feels like a loss of control.

Those of us already dealing with stress that makes us feel powerless may avoid looking too closely at our office's numbers in case our suspicions are confirmed because then we need to take on what may be an exhausting and uncomfortable process of confronting the one stealing from the till, replacing them, and coping with the financial and emotional harm the thief leaves in their wake.

Some dentists feel so emotionally ill-equipped to manage that conflict that they keep employees they know are stealing from them. Keeping the staff member feels easier than the changes they need to make in their systems and staff.

This will only lead to more costs because dishonest employees cost everyone. Here's how: First, when an employee steals from you, they don't just take your money; they take your trust, too. It's emotionally costly. Second, having a team member who steals affects the culture at work. That kind of dishonesty and lack of accountability creates a toxic culture that motivates good employees to move on to better, safer places. That leaves you holding the bag as you try to cope with keeping your practice afloat while also dealing with staff turnover and increasingly less functional employees.

I know it's tempting to avoid pain when you're already in pain, but this is something that will only get worse. It's very important to reach out and get whatever emotional support you need in addressing this issue in your professional life. Reaching out neutralizes shame, which is draining and leads to isolation. Prolonged stress in isolation will burn you out. Combat shame and isolation with help from a trusted mental health professional and peers. Chances are, you know plenty of dentists in the same boat.

When you have the right support, you'll be ready to follow through on tackling embezzlement from a practical standpoint.

Embezzlement Recovery and Protection Strategies

Nobody is totally immune from theft or embezzlement. If you suspect that something is not quite right with your office finances, chances are, you're right. The silver lining to the commonality of this problem is that you can know that being stolen from doesn't reflect on you, personally. It's an industry-wide problem that affects all clinical specialties. It's not about you being naive; it's a problem of opaque accounting. This leads to the next solution: creating crystal clear accounting systems.

Remove human error where possible

There are many software programs available for dental offices that can catch small financial errors (whether they're accidental or deliberate) and aggregate the data to notify you of growing discrepancies.

Set these programs and apps up to fit your practice. Limit employee access rights to ledger programs—for instance, you can permit staff to add and edit items but not delete them. Check all the employee practice management software account accesses to make sure they don't have the ability to change the fee schedule, collections, and/or write-offs.

These software programs can run audit reports, which is invaluable for determining the state of your till and for providing evidence should you need to confront or fire a staff member.

Manage the money and the mail yourself or separate these duties

Make sure only practice owners retrieve and open mail and write or stamp checks.

Make sure all the checks patients write are made out to you, both by telling the patients and by adding specific, written instructions to your office's bills.

Pay the office's bills yourself. If it involves writing a check, do it yourself. In my office, we don't accept cash. If you do, I wouldn't recommend accepting cash from patients of more than $100.

Don't give credit cards to any staff. If you must, have a second credit card with a balance limit of $500. Make sure you have software and mobile apps to track purchases and card usage so that you can double-check every credit card transaction with a day sheet and to check for suspicious activities.

Know the Numbers

Checking and making sure your day sheet balances with your deposit and batch report is incredibly useful and a basic minimum standard in any business. Hire auditors and watch for red flags. Some employees seem like the perfect employee because they are staying late and not taking vacations, but these could very well be the ones stealing from you. Also, watch out for those employees who get territorial over their workstation and don't allow other employees to use their computer.

There is no substitute for oversight. You need to check your numbers and understand what to check them against. Some dentists resist this because it's more work, but keeping track on a regular basis is way less work than the aftermath of embezzlement.

Again, this may sound like a lot of work, but I assure you that it's way less work (and less upsetting) than scrambling to uncover the damage in the wake of employee embezzlement. You can't totally prevent it but can minimize the opportunities. If you're interested in learning more about this issue, I'd encourage you to check out my Deals for Dentists podcast episode with David Harris, the CEO of Prosperident, who investigates dental office embezzlement.

Insurance

My least favorite part of dentistry is having to deal with money. I like making it, don't get me wrong, but I don't like talking about it. I wish I could make what I make and let everything be free.

—DR. JOSH P.

Managing insurance is really stressful for several reasons:

It's complicated

Every insurance plan is different, and they're often deliberately obfuscatory.

It's always changing

Insurance is always changing, which means it's not only complicated, it's always newly complicated. In-network providers find new ways to save themselves money by declining, delaying, or downgrading payments. Keeping up on the latest insurance codes and maintaining excellent records of all contacts made with insurance reps and claims is a part-time job at least and one that adds significantly to office overhead without bringing in revenue the way our dental hygiene teams do. Sometimes it can be frustrating to need to reallocate needed resources.

It's not even really insurance

The problem with dental insurance is that it's not really insurance—it's just a plan put in place to offset predictable dental expenses. Most of us are more familiar with a different insurance paradigm that obligates an insurance company towards more coverage than dental insurance companies usually provide, which makes everyone predictably unhappy.

It creates an adversarial relationship between patients and providers

Every dentist I know likes to be able to help people and relieve pain, and when paperwork and lack of funds stand in the way, it's emotionally draining. Or like when an insurance company will pay for a bridge but not an implant even though the patient and I have decided the implant would be the better option.

Because of this, we often experience insurance companies as the bad guys who fail to support our patients, their clients, in getting the work done that we know they need. And then, when insurance companies leave the patient to pay for everything out of pocket, we may feel like the bad guy when we need to charge a fair price for that work. Some dentists will give a discount or completely write off the procedure's copay to help the patient out. Not only that, often, negative reviews on social media are due to miscommunications about insurance benefits.

Insurance Strategies

Phone-side work supports chairside work

You need someone in your office who has the interpersonal and organizational skills to maintain all the latest codes, claims, and contact info for whatever insurance you decide to take. Sometimes older practices resist committing to this because people dislike change, and those unaware of the volatility of dental insurance may not understand the importance of devoting a portion of an office's overhead towards constant insurance management. If you don't want to do it in-house, you can outsource insurance verification and management. There are plenty of companies that offer this as a service.

Stay current on the constant changes

Dental insurance plans are constantly changing, and you need to know what's going on in order to decide which insurance companies are best for you. These changes will affect insurance codes, deductibles, days of payment, and more.

Patient education

Like I said before, dental insurance is a planned offset for basic dental maintenance. Patients who are more familiar with the medical insurance model will naturally expect more coverage for dental procedures and therefore, will likely resist paying out-of-pocket for needed procedures. If you can reset these expectations and help patients see what an investment in their health needed dental procedures can be, that can take the sting out of what feels like insurance companies depriving you and your patients of expected support.

Discount Membership Plans

I am a huge advocate for in-house membership plans which offer patients without dental insurance a discount on their treatment.

This is both an emotional and a practical solution. Practically speaking, it meets patients where they are and offers more flexibility for them to plan the costs of dental care into their own budgets. This treats dental work as the serious investment it is, at least as important as other things requiring payment plans.

Emotionally, it means we have the relief of offering options, especially to patients with difficult personal circumstances. This addresses the stress we feel as providers of needed clinical care when

THE STRESS-FREE DENTIST

we want to have an economically sustainable way to help those with fewer financial resources. Membership plans are freeing. There are no strings attached, and they can be very simple to implement. If you don't want to do it yourself, there are many companies that can handle all of the behind-the-scenes management for a fee.

They are also a great source of recurring revenue. We charge a yearly fee, but some offices run the patient's card monthly, like a membership with Netflix or Amazon.

Here is my In-Office Membership Plan at the time of writing this book:

Acton Dental Membership Plan

Finally...

You can get our unique Acton Dental Membership Plan for a low annual membership fee.

Our membership plan is designed to provide greater access to quality dental care at an affordable price, as well as a discount on other restorative and emergency services.

Check out our Coverage section for a list of the benefits you will enjoy as a member of our plan.

To enroll, fill out the form to the right or call one of our friendly front desk team and tell them you want the peace of mind our Membership Plan can give you.

Coverage

Diagnostic Care

Service	Plan Discount
Comprehensive Exam	100%
New Patient/Initial Visit	100%
2 Annual Exams (Non-Emergency)	100%
4 Bite Wing X-Rays	100%
Additional Routine X-Rays (Non-Emergency)	100%
Complete Series X-Rays or Panorex (One per 5 years)	100%
Consultations	100%

Preventative Dentistry

Prophylaxis (two cleanings per year)	100%
Fluoride (two treatments per year up to age 16)	100%
Oral Cancer Screening (two per year)	100%
Sealants	15%
Scaling and Root Planing	15%
Additional Periodontal Maintenance Cleanings	15%

All Other Procedures

Fillings	15%
Posts and Core Buildups	15%
Oral Surgery	15%
Crowns	15%
Veneers	15%
Dentures and Partials	15%
Implants	15%
3D Imaging CBCT	15%
Whitening	15%
Night Guards	15%
Emergency Exam and X-Rays	15%

If you don't see a service listed, please call us at

www.actondental.com

Please Fill Out and Return This Form Today to Start Coverage

First Name
Last Name
Middle Initial
Home Address
City   State   Zip
Phone
Email
Date of Birth   Female/Male

Spouse First Name
Last Name
Middle Initial
Date of Birth   Female/Male

Child First Name
Date of Birth   Daughter/Son

Child First Name
Date of Birth   Daughter/Son

Child First Name
Date of Birth   Daughter/Son

Child First Name
Date of Birth   Daughter/Son

Enrollment Period _____ to _____

Return the completed form to Acton Dental Associates

DON'T LET THE MONEY BURN YOU

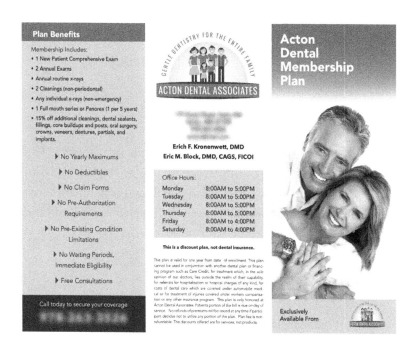

Budgets, Goals, and Benchmarks

Budgets are both frustrating and comforting because budgets promise the illusion of certainty and control. We know the numbers matter and very much want to exercise that control.

However, the only thing predictable about life is its unpredictability. Budgets are, basically, predictions of the future, but often things happen that nobody could have predicted. Business ownership will teach anyone that, and the COVID-19-related or other previous economic recession-related upheaval has been a stark reminder of this truth.

Projections and reality only sometimes match. This mismatch often brings a sense of frustration and failure and possibly shame. It's not hard to want to avoid anything that brings those feelings by either avoiding working on one's budget or by white-knuckling the numbers to no avail.

Here's what to do about it

The first step is to have budgets, goals, and benchmarks. Get together with your bookkeeper, accountant, or financial advisor and start formulating a concrete plan. Goals and benchmarks can't just be in your head. They have to be written down and said out loud.

Drop the shame

Remember that hardly any of us in practice went to business school and that we're learning on the job. One of the lessons business schools teach is that most businesses have to ditch their original strategic plans to cope with unforeseen conditions.[19]

If your office's budget doesn't match your forecast, that's actually the most predictable forecast of all. Sometimes that fear of failure can get us stuck in emotional patterns around money. Half of all money management is really emotional management, and the sooner you can see and accept your feelings around money, the sooner you can separate the two issues and solve each in a productive way.

Connect with other dentists—they're probably dealing with the same problem, and you'll see that you're not alone, and you're

---

[19] Georgetown Chamber of Commerce & Industry. 2021. *An Agile Approach to Budgeting for Uncertain Times*. [online] Available at: <https://gcci.gy/an-agile-approach-to-budgeting-for-uncertain-times/> [Accessed 28 February 2021].

okay. Knowing you're not alone can help you manage the emotional part of financial stress and leave more energy you can use to move forward into solving the financial part of the problem.

I use software called Dental Intel that helps me not only track collections and accounts receivable but certain KPI's (Key Performance Indicators) to track things like same-day production percentage, production per hour, production per visit, perio and treatment diagnosis percentage, perio and treatment acceptance rate percentage, hygiene and new patient reappointment rates, and more.

I explain to the staff that this is not to keep score but to see who needs help in a specific area so I can get them the help they need. Sometimes the data will show that it's the dentists that need the improvement.

Get flexible

If budgets and goals are inflexible, then it's easy to obsess over its accuracy. Add flexibility to your process—make sure you can adjust your long-term forecast every quarter, or month, or week, if need be. This will give you and your team a great way to view unforeseen events as valuable lessons instead of costly mistakes and to adjust your budget around your hard-won expertise.

Use the right-sized data sets

I recommend examining budgets monthly or quarterly as opposed to semi-annually and annually. Compare this year's May to last year's May. Or this year's quarter to last year's quarter. How did it compare, and what needs improvement?

Set Benchmarks

I personally like to have goals set for my personal and business set for one, two, five, and ten-year increments. I like to keep an eye on the short term and the long term. If my collections were low or my overhead was up. Why? I need to figure out what happened and make a plan to improve.

> *"It's important to have a therapist or have a coach, somebody who can help you get through times of crisis, so you don't worry about things so much. You can stay focused on meeting your bottom line financially and taking good care of your patients."*
>
> –DR. ALDEN CASS

ROI versus ROF (Return on Investment versus Return on Fun)

As dentists, we do need to pay attention to our overhead and break-even points, but I'm a big advocate for return on fun (ROF) over return on investment (ROI). If there is an expensive piece of equipment that may not have the return on investment but makes you love going to work every day, then you should buy it. My intraoral scanner is a perfect example. Is it cheaper to just take regular poly-vinyl impressions? Sure, but do I love scanning, and does it make me and the staff look forward to doing crowns and night guards? Absolutely. It is also impressive to the patient and something we can use for marketing. If it makes your life better and easier, pull the trigger—it will pay off as ROF.

Another example is my digital implant workflow. Implant dentistry is one of my most enjoyable and least stressful procedures I do nowadays. Sure, it would be cheaper just to take a Pan or a PA and free hand the implant surgery. But I purchased a CBCT and 3-D printer and look forward to digitally planning my implant surgeries. These are not cheap investments, but they have a great ROF. I take a CBCT, scan the patient's mouth, and virtually plan and place the implant. I then 3-D print my surgical guide. I do this for every implant case, and the implant surgery is so much quicker, efficient, more accurate, less traumatic for the patient, but most importantly, so much fun. To me, it is worth every penny I spent on these big-ticket equipment items.

Summary

- Know your numbers. If numbers worry you, hire someone trustworthy to help you understand and work them.
- Expecting perfection means planning to be stressed out. Persistence is better than perfect.
- Use benchmarks to bridge the gap between budget forecasts and business reality.
- If you're thinking about transitioning to owner, evaluate the prospective practice's financial state and your own emotional and physical state.
- Quick daily audits can help prevent embezzlement.
- Consider ROF versus ROI

CHAPTER 8
BUSINESS MANAGEMENT WITH BOUNDARIES

It's really hard to invest so much personally and financially in dental school, only to graduate and realize that after years of focusing on achievement and the ability to put knowledge into practice, I had no business management to put into my practice. When I graduated from dental school, I did not yet know how to communicate with patients, how to perform many procedures, and I really didn't know how to run a business.

As an associate, I just had to show up and do my thing. I worked hard to treat the patients on my schedule, and then I went home. I didn't need to know the numbers or how to manage the budget. I didn't have to deal with staff members calling in sick or crying. I didn't know how insurance worked or how copays were calculated, and I definitely didn't know how to train a team member or how to hire or fire one.

I worked as an associate a long time before transitioning to owner because I didn't feel ready to become the CEO of a company. I struggled already with people-pleasing, and it takes firm boundaries to manage a staff in a practice. I worried about making sure my clinical skills were up to par and needed to learn how to maintain my own training before I could guide training for someone else. I needed time because I had to learn all of this on the go. Before I could be the CEO of a company, I had to learn how to be the CEO of myself. I needed time to learn all of this on the go—and, along the way, I also learned how to be the CEO of myself by solving my burnout.

Burnout isn't great, but I view it now as a terrific learning opportunity. I was forced to learn how to solve important problems around communication, priorities, and accountability, which I was then able to apply in managing my growing practice.

Here's the great thing about burnout: it shows you your hotspots. The pain it brings will pinpoint what you need to work on in order to know how to work.

My experience with burnout showed me that my hotspot was anxiety. That taught me that I needed to take care of my anxiety through therapy, the right combination of prescribed medications, and by creating processes that are ready-made responses for some of my worst fears. This process of healing also taught me how to work on myself. That laid a foundation for knowing how to work on a practice.

As you identify and address your hotspots, you'll probably find that you, too, are laying a foundation for personal and then professional growth. Solving your own inner issues is crucial to making your business flourish as you take on your next challenge: using burnout recovery principles to help your business grow in a healthy way. As you address your burnout, you'll find that you'll do far better in business which will then lead to growth. It's crucial to solve your own issues so that you can flourish because as you do, your business will, too—which will present you with the next challenge: how to use burnout recovery principles and healthy boundaries to help your business grow in a healthy way.

During the last ten years, several doctors have told me their intention was to hire a competent office manager to run the business side because they *"just want to do dentistry."* Of course, they do! They've devoted most of the last decade to learning dentistry, and they want to hit the ground running to help patients. Still, I find it shocking when I hear them say this because it shows their disconnect that dental practices are businesses, and as business owners, they're responsible for running them. I also meet doctors who have been in practice for a number of years who still don't understand the basics of business ownership. Their approach is, *"If there's money in the bank at the end of the month, I'm doing OK!"* [20]

Growth: A Great Problem To Have

In the beginning, management and quality control seem easy. If we're associates, we leave it up to the owner, and there are very few people to deal with. This is especially true for those of us in solo practices.

When we make the leap to owner, it's a huge purchase, gambling on our ability to run that practice in a way that takes care of patients' dental needs while also taking care of your and your staff's financial needs. We make this leap because there is so much to be gained—but, of course, there's a lot to lose, too, if we don't address the stress that causes burnout.

As your business scales up, it becomes more important to make sure you have boundaries in place that will set standards all employees must meet and the processes they should use to meet them.

---

[20] Greer, RDH, BS, A., 2018. *The desperate need for business education in dentistry.* [online] DentistryIQ. Available at: <https://www.dentistryiq.com/practice-management/practice-management-tips/article/16367683/the-desperate-need-for-business-education-in-dentistry> [Accessed 28 February 2021].

I hope that many of my readers who are students, grads, and associates will be able to start building a burnout-proof business from the ground up. For those of us who are already owners, when we start to figure these things out, don't worry—there's hope for us, too. The improvements we make within will help us make those improvements in our practice, so everyone can thrive.

In this chapter, we're going to go over each burnout stressor and talk about the management strategies that I've found helpful to change that stressor into a strength, with practical examples of what this looks like in my practice.

Business Management and Burnout

What situations create burnout?

- Lack of control
- Unclear job expectations
- Lack of social support
- Lack of feeling appreciated
- Perceived lack of achievement
- Work-life imbalance
- Dysfunctional workplace dynamics

Let's talk about how each one manifests and what to do to solve it as a manager.

Problem: Work-life imbalance

Solutions: Decide on priorities, set boundaries around work time, and lead by example.

How it Manifests

When there's a serious work-life imbalance, you'll know it because people take work home and bring personal problems into the office. People are increasingly anxious and depressed, and everyone's struggling to get the exercise and good food they need to be healthy. You're lonely, or staff mention they're lonely. There seems to be a lot of illness and absenteeism. And, finally, everyone seems busy, and yet nothing seems to get done. Remember my Sweatpants to Scrubs Equilibrium theory? You're constantly wanting to escape to your sweatpants during scrub-time, and you can't stop thinking about work when you're in your sweatpants.

Work-Life Imbalance: Solutions

Set Priorities

When everything is a top priority, it means people run around like crazy, yet things aren't getting done well or at all. Time and energy are finite resources, and as the leader, you have the power to help people use them wisely by determining which things are priorities. Everything can't be number one.

Have set work hours—and stick to them

It's too easy to fall into patterns of workaholism. Even if you talk a good game about taking time off, if you don't lead by example, you will not solve this problem. People who care about their jobs watch for cues on how to fit in with their workplace, and if the boss never takes time off, then that sends a powerful message to staff that they shouldn't, either.

Take time off. It's a win/win. I get it. You are neck-deep in bills and debt. But taking time off is like mental payment for your brain. Sure, when you are away from the office, you aren't producing, but when you return from your break, you will come back more energized and produce more chairside dentistry than if you didn't take time off.

Make sure you and your team understand how to find the equilibrium in the sweatpants and scrubs fight club. You can give 100 percent when you are in your scrubs to your work, and when you get home, you can give 100 percent while in your sweatpants if you recognize there is a problem, ask for help, and get comfortable in your own skin.

Problem: Lack of safety

Solution: Set clear rules that everyone is held accountable to and a culture that values people's feelings. Write it down and get your staff on board. If you don't know what you want your practice culture to be, then how do you expect your staff to perform?

How it manifests

Bullying in a workplace often goes unnoticed because it can be a subtle, slow process of growing manipulation and intimidation. Because those who target others are skilled at hiding it or making it look like concern or being helpful, it can be difficult to detect.

Real bullying looks less like a schoolyard brawl and more like manipulation, gossip, threats, and exclusion of certain team members—so, take notice if one of your staff members invites everyone but one to their party. Bullies also minimize or dismiss concerns or feelings, play dumb, or change the subject instead of addressing things that need to be resolved directly.

If someone withholds information, blames others, takes credit for their achievements, or makes it impossible for people to succeed, then they are bullying people. Gossip and whispering about people behind their backs, especially in a critical and demeaning way, is also bullying.

Feeling unsafe at work is a huge reason why people burn out and why good people leave bad practices. Nobody wants to be unsafe, and everyone deserves to feel like there is a minimum standard of respect and accountability where they work.

Lack of Safety: Solutions

Keep your eyes peeled

People who are being bullied often appear tired, confused, frustrated, fearful, may seem overly emotional or avoid coworkers or leaders. Understand that staff may be too scared to tell you. A lot of dentists are oblivious to what is really going on with the culture in their office.

Create policy and hold everyone to it

Create a policy and establish a code of conduct that specifically forbids this kind of behavior. Train everyone on what basic respect looks like and how to show it, and make this code of conduct training a major part of hiring. Train your managers on how to recognize bullying and how to report it.

Listen

Provide a confidential way for employees to report being bullied or feeling unsafe at work so that they can let you know about issues that need your attention without fear of reprisal. Make sure you follow up on these complaints—take them seriously and investigate them. Train your managers as well. Taking feelings seriously and acting on them is what lays a foundation for a culture of trust and respect.

Document

Document all incidents you hear about from employees or witnesses. When I struggle to know what to do about an employee, a paper trail helps me evaluate what to do next. For instance, you can have a policy that three documented incidents will result in firing that employee. It helps to have procedures to fall back on. If you don't already, seek the expertise of an HR consultant to help you set up processes and procedures for reporting.

Problem: Lack of Control

Solution: communication, grievance box, no micromanagement

How it manifests

People want to feel in control of their lives, and when they don't, their motivation drops. You may notice that your staff is acting apathetic or resentful. They also seem to complain a lot.

You may also notice that you're worn out or that you feel like you have to do everyone else's jobs for them. When that happens, it's a sign that you're micromanaging and need to reset healthy boundaries and turn control of some things over to those employees.

Lack of control: Solutions

Trust your staff

Dentists are detail-oriented and have specific ways we want tasks to be completed. But it's imperative we learn to delegate. Make sure your front desk is sticking to the scheduling system, provide the training they need, but then let them do the job you're paying them to do. People know when they're trusted and when their boss is hovering. Distrust breeds confused and unhappy team members, which is the opposite of the empowered, independent thinkers and workers you want.

Good Vibes Only

I put up a sign in my office that says "Good Vibes Only." Our rule is, if you present with a complaint, you have to bring a solution. This is an empowering approach; it shows I trust my team to come up with solutions.

Have a Designated Place to Go with Concerns

While I want solutions, it's important to keep an eye on problems. If someone has a grievance, they know they can go to our office manager with any issue.

Support your staff

You like improving; you want your practice to improve, too. The best way to encourage people to help you with that is to hire people who expect to improve as well. Set goals with staff members for what they'd like to work on in themselves and as a team.

Problem: Unclear job expectations

Solution: Training, clear communication, manuals, and flowcharts.

How it manifests

When job expectations are unclear, what it looks like is that your staff are frequently underprepared or fighting over the same things. There's who owns the practices, and then there's who runs it, and sometimes it's not the same thing.

Meanwhile, you notice tasks being left undone, and it's a struggle to get people to do them. You hired people who seemed competent, but tasks you feel are simple still aren't completed to your liking. In places where expectations are unclear, you will have wildly varying results from your people—some of them will overdo it and seem stressed out all the time, while others seem lazy and consistently underperform. You frequently feel frustrated with how out of sync they are, especially with your expectations as an owner—working with them chairside is much harder than it has to be, and even the simplest administration tasks always seem to need your input. Meanwhile, everyone keeps coming to you with their problems!

Unclear job expectations: Solutions

Get everyone on the same page—literally

Did dental school train us in behavioral sciences? Of course not. I highly recommend a professional HR (human resources) company to create an office handbook that is customized to your office and state laws. They can also help with clearly written job descriptions.

Communicate clearly

Are you training your people to do their tasks well? How do you know when they're ready to fly solo? Prevent burnout by having reasonable expectations and communicating them clearly. This may mean correcting an employee. Tell them calmly and civilly what's wrong and how to fix it, and then when they do, recognize that. Or if you have an office manager, then delegate these duties to them.

Create a flowchart—and stick to it

Post it even, if you can, in order to keep everyone in the office accountable.

Many offices have an "official" flowchart of jobs and tasks. You know, the one that is posted on the wall, but nobody lives by, and the "unofficial" one that actually gets things done, though sometimes in a dysfunctional manner. This leads to rivalries, manipulation, drama, and resentment.

Don't let that start in your office. Make it clear who manages which tasks and which people, and make sure everyone else knows it, too.

If you have an office manager who's supposed to be handling supply or managing the scheduling, and you make that clear, then you should no longer have to handle random supply or scheduling issues from your staff. That is your OM's job.

Create and automate workflows.

I created checklists for our assistants and staff to follow for tasks like prepping rooms and opening and closing the practice for the day's business. We also have documents and easy-to-follow instructions for handoff from the back office to the front desk. I have developed a system of automation for my staff and myself while doing procedures. When systems and procedures are automatic, it creates less guesswork, and everyone knows what to do, which creates a lot less stress.

I love these things! They're so clear, and they're all in writing, and it's very easy to see if tasks are done or undone. I'll include some sample workflows and checklists in my final chapter.

Keep everyone informed.

Make sure that everyone is on the same page by ensuring everyone gets the same information at the same time. We use email to inform everyone of things in writing and to post meeting notes. We have a few large dry erase boards in the office—one with the staff calendar and another with upcoming events, and a third for fun things like posting patient reviews or giving shout-outs to other staff members.

Now we are having our office meetings through zoom, which can be recorded and sent to staff who were or were not there.

Problem: Lack of support at work

Solution: systems, ergonomics, training

How it manifests:

People keep complaining about back, eye, or hand/wrist strain. Your staff keeps making mistakes with things like scheduling, handoffs to the front desk, billing, or prepping rooms. The energy in your office feels like the tide—sometimes things are full and frantic and overwhelming, punctuated by doldrums of ten minutes or more at a time when everyone is twiddling their thumbs. You and your team often feel nervous, stressed, and overwhelmed by basic aspects of their jobs, and there's constant conflict having to do with your office, your supplies. It seems like everyone's really tired or running late, and you felt embarrassed in front of a patient due to lack of preparation or follow-through with your staff.

Lack of work support: Solutions

Create an onboarding process for new and existing staff

You need an onboarding process that takes new hires and trains them to become a helpful part of the team. It can be hard to know how to pace training, especially for those of us who never had training in how to train! Focus on adding an additional task each week, and lead with recognition of things done well. Yes, you can point out errors, but do so in a way that helps people feel respected and encouraged by pointing out what they're doing well, too, and that you have confidence in them and are there to support them.

Check your systems

I cannot stress this one enough—a practice is only as good as its people, and its people are as effective as its systems. When systems are clunky, people stop using them, and then the whole practice flails. Make sure your staff sticks to the systems by training them in using them, offering support in continuing to use them, and making those systems something that can be relied on to work at your operating volume.

If you decide to change systems, consider asking an expert to evaluate them and recommend what to change in what order. Make changes slowly. I made the mistake of trying to overhaul too fast; it just caused more stress.

Delegate the task

One of the biggest causes of stress in a dental practice is a disorganized, poorly balanced schedule. You need to balance your activity level with production goals. Consider making one of your team members the scheduling coordinator, and get very clear with them on procedure times. The clearer you are, the better they can support you. Delegation is the key to happiness. I love to train and help my team feel valued, and I can spend more time doing the things I enjoy. I delegate as much as legally allowed in the state of Massachusetts.

Problem: Lack of social support

Solution: Boost morale, have a daily huddle

How it manifests

The staff doesn't really seem in sync, and they don't talk much to each other. It's hard to get them to speak to you, too. Patients seem quiet and bored. Nobody is on the same page, and you've noticed that you have to keep repeating the same information to different people. It takes so much time to talk to people!

Lack of social support: Solutions

Spruce up your office

Humans love beauty, and we dentists also love cleanliness. How does your office look? How does it smell and feel?

I had everyone take turns sitting in the patient chairs so we could all see and feel what patients see and feel, and I tried to make improvements to that experience where we could with cleaning, repair, and decoration. We've got some great ceiling panels!

Sometimes an improvement in office aesthetics can improve office morale. Who wouldn't love working in a clean and inviting office?

Show appreciation and respect to your staff

Dentistry is all about connection, and it's great to help patients and staff make those connections. I did this by putting up a fun staff bio wall that I called "Let's Taco About Our Staff!".

Create opportunities for peer support

You can't force coworkers to be friends, but you can definitely make it easier for them to connect. I plan outings to boost staff morale once a month, just for fun. Our activities have included things like painting together or carving pumpkins for Halloween.

Morning huddle

This is the five to ten-minute meeting we hold every morning before the day starts. Make it clear that huddle topics are limited to getting everyone on the same page for the day's schedule and finding out who needs what help for which procedures or patients. This is a great time to give shout-outs, too—praise is nice, but praise given in front of witnesses is awesome. It's a great way to start the day with a little boost and direction for everyone. It's also a great way to create opportunities and fill the schedule or make the day more profitable and efficient. For example, a hygienist will review their schedule and give a report like, "My first patient, Mrs. Jones, has a birthday today, so let's all give her a warm, happy birthday welcome. She's also due for an FMX. Can someone help me take that for her? She also needs two fillings, and Dr. Block has some time today. Can we see if we can fill that slot?"

Problem: Lack of appreciation and achievement

Solution: One on ones, setting goals

How it manifests:

People feel like no matter how much they do, it's never enough. People seem to be underperforming, and you're either having to point out what they're doing wrong, or you're avoiding telling them. They seem discouraged anyway.

Lack of achievement: Solutions

Check for fit

As the leader, it's your job to put people in the best position to win. If they're not succeeding, don't just attribute it to laziness, stupidity, or failure in hiring. If they're not doing well on phones, maybe they'd be better off working in another role, like marketing. The important thing is not to try and hammer a square peg into a round hole. If someone's personality is not a good fit for a certain job, then why try to force them into that position? It's going to create stress for them and their co-workers. Instead, put them in the job where they will succeed. Everyone will be happier, and the practice will run smoother.

Deal with failure constructively

Give clear, honest feedback on what employees did wrong, but take care to do it professionally and respectfully, with a focus on what they specifically need to do differently in the future.

Set achievable goals

When all goals seem too hard, it's easier not to have any at all. Break processes down into achievable steps and recognize when people make those steps.

Give positive feedback

Anxiety can make people paranoid about their job being in danger or how unhappy their boss is with them. You can't fix someone else's anxiety, but you can refuse to feed it by making sure to give positive professional feedback. Meet with your staff on a regular basis to figure out what the best goals are for them so that they know how to do well and that they're capable of it.

Executive Staff Check-ins (ESCs)

People crave feedback. One-on-one meetings with either you or the office manager are a great way to systemize giving helpful feedback and moving forward—and you can learn a lot as well. I include more notes about how to do these in the final chapter.

Staff reviews are also important for dentists in your office. Associates, especially young new grads, want to know how they are doing. I remember my second or third year as an associate in the practice; I had no idea what the owners thought of me or my work. There wasn't a review process in place to give me feedback. One day we were at a local study club, and I overheard one of the owners talking about me saying, "He's going to be a long-term fixture in the office and is a great dentist." Until that moment, I had no idea they felt that way.

Problem: Dysfunctional workplace dynamics

Solution: Hiring, firing, and managing staff turnover.

How it manifests:

It's miserable at work, and people are talking to each other less and less.

There's that one person at work that everyone tiptoes around or who always brings their problems into work. You keep having issues with scheduling because there are two people who refuse to get along, and that resentment comes out and affects your patients. You dread having to find a new front desk person—you just replaced them with someone who had a great resume, but already there've been problems with the handoff.

There are people who act out and get away with it, and everyone knows it.

Check the culture

It can be tempting to think things are all in our heads, especially when it has to do with other people's feelings. Conduct a culture check using the questionnaire in Chapter 7: Office Culture: Is Yours Toxic? Does your culture check out? Or does it have signs of toxicity? Healthy practices have teamwork and productivity and are positive places to be. If people dread coming in to work, then you have a problem.

Identify the bad actors

This is where it's crucial to have a system of documenting incidents and grievances and a solid OM who can help manage these issues. If you don't have those systems, start changing that now. I hired a professional HR company to help me with this. Especially when your staff starts to grow, HR becomes more complex. A quality HR company is worth every penny for its services.

Don't pick favorites

It can be tempting to favor an ally, especially when work feels like a battleground. As the leader, you can't afford to do that. It's easy for the dentist to favor your chairside assistant over the other employees. If you do this, it won't go unnoticed. The staff will start to resent you and your assistant. It's best to treat everyone equally. I also don't recommend having out-of-work events with just some of the staff. It is all or nothing when it comes to staff and after-work events.

Get comfortable with hiring—and firing

These are both things that scare people growing into business management, but they're practicable skills and can be helpful in turning a toxic practice around.

I make sure to hire on cultural fit and attitude—we can always train people to work in dentistry, but you can't train a person to be kind, energetic, great with people, or naturally organized.

And when it comes to firing people, many people hate to do it, especially if that employee has been there a long time. It helps me to remember that if you keep toxic employees, soon that's all you'll have. The ones with boundaries and self-respect will leave. Let go of the ones who aren't a good fit for your office. They'll be happier somewhere else, and you will be happier without them. And when you fire them, remember to be clear and quick. Don't beat around the bush or gradually lead up to it.

Making Changes

All of these solutions have something in common: they require making changes.

When I started assessing my practice, I did so much reading, and researching, and investigating. I realized how much better the practice could be and how much better our work lives could be, too, and I couldn't wait to get started. I was tired of the status quo—it was time for the next level! So I jumped in and started making changes ... and ran into a major roadblock with my staff.

They resisted these changes, complaining about them, and were really reluctant to try new things. I was frustrated, yes, but then I realized this was my fault.

What I failed to do was to disclose what I was trying to do and explain their part and what I would do to support them through these changes.

I realized that what I should have done was hold a meeting with everyone, where I would explain my new role and all the changes I would make, get everyone on board, and then move forward slowly.

Change can be really hard for a lot of people, especially if they already feel ignored or like they don't have a lot of control. You need to get your team on board.

To get your team on board, you need to have a clear vision. If you don't understand what your goals are, how can you communicate them to the team? One way you can get a clearer vision of where you want to be is to find examples of dentists who you'd like to "grow up" to be.

I based my vision on a couple of great examples of doctors I worked for as an associate. I observed them while they were in their element and working with their team. Every single person knew their role and how their job served the team's larger goals. If they weren't willing to be a functional team member, they were fired. There was no dead weight; there were no emotional vampires. Best of all, the person who handled the process wasn't the dentists; it was the office manager. There were clear procedures for assessing job performance, addressing problems, and finally, firing. Because the procedures were clear and known, the dentists didn't have to be involved in every single human resources decision.

When I talked to one of them one day, he said, "Someone was let go the other day because they didn't have the right attitude for the team, and I just found out about it now." How cool is that? He could be confident the team leaders knew what was best for the office, and when a new hire didn't fit, the office manager could see it and let them go during the three-month trial period, saving huge amounts of grief down the line.

These dentists made delegation work by seeing themselves as CEOs. They handled the big picture, but there was a clear chain of command, and everyone knew where they fell in it. They had good people in the right positions and clear expectations. That meant that they could safely delegate, knowing that the team could function organically. Instead of having to think about every single step of every process all day, the CEO could concentrate on the things that only he could do.

It was the difference between consciously deciding when and how to breathe in and out and trusting your lungs to work for you, as needed. If you had to plan each heartbeat and breath, you'd go crazy! There'd be no time to do anything but the bare minimum of not dying. By having clear procedures and chains of command, these doctors could function like our brains do—free to learn things and make big plans because we can trust that the various body systems are doing their parts.

Solidify your vision

Find some way to visualize where you want your practice to be. What does it look like? What does it feel like working there? Where have you seen and felt this before? Use books, mentors, and fellow dentists for guidance on how to really nail down your inspiration so that you can properly prioritize and plan the changes you need to make.

Get buy-in by sharing the Why

If you can involve your people in assessing and solving problems, and they feel heard and valued and informed, they're more likely to support the changes you make. When people know the Why, they're better able to contribute to the How.

Make a plan

Many people plant their heels when faced with the unknown. Make a plan, so people all know what you're working towards together. Is it a better scheduling system? Is it better room prep? Is it staff morale? Help people know what to expect so that they feel like you're giving them a fair chance to do their best.

Prioritize changes and go slow

Change is hard, so focus on the most important things first. If your schedule is chaotic, focus on that. If you have out-of-control drama from one of your staff members, then replacing them is the priority.

Set achievable goals

Break your changes into achievable pieces, and then recognize everyone's contributions when you reach those goals. It's easier to get buy-in when improvements look like a regular human can do it.

Build on your strengths

People love being able to be competent. What is your staff already really good at? How can you connect needed changes to their current skills? This turns change from a scary experience with the loss of control into a fun challenge that helps people grow.

Bring in support

Consider hiring an expert to help assess your practice, prioritize needed changes, and support you and your staff through the needed retraining and conflict resolution that will take your practice to the next level.

We want to enjoy work, and a key part of work is feeling like it's worth it. For many of us, that means growing in revenue and size. We all want our practices to succeed, but if you don't have personnel and systems dialed in, growth can be stressful or even destructive. When you scale up, solutions that were sufficient may no longer be, and big problems become even bigger.

Some stress is unavoidable but can be planned for. Burnout is a sign of runaway stress and stress factors and an indication it's time to take a detailed look under the hood of your practice to see what changes you need to make so it can run more smoothly.

A solid, fire-resistant practice has the right team, knows the numbers, focuses on its personal and clinical strengths.

Preparing for predictable stresses in advance is a great way to protect yourself against future burnout.

Key Takeaways

- Don't pick favorites. Doing so will negatively impact your work environment.
- Don't gossip about employees—ever. You are the boss; act like one.
- Make sure all policies are in writing.
- Make sure your written policies include proper use of your practices' computers and phones.
- Include disciplinary steps in an employee handbook, no matter how small your practice is.
- Deal with inappropriate behavior immediately, and make sure you're providing a safe work environment.
- Have an open-door policy for your employees to be able to come and share concerns.
- Have a grievance box that employees can put notes in. Have this box in a discreet place, like a breakroom or the bathroom.
- Do something! Your team needs strong leadership. If you aren't able to provide it, then find a business coach who can help you to develop that skill.

CHAPTER 9

I BEAT BURNOUT — AND YOU CAN, TOO

Burnout is common among dentists. I challenge you to ask any of your peers if they are feeling stressed or burned out right now. Chances are good someone you know is experiencing some level of burnout.

For students, grads, and associates: The most important thing to know is that if you're not burned out yet, be proactive to stop it before it starts. Now is the time to address your anxiety and depression, to learn how to set boundaries and communicate, and to make sure you cultivate a work/life balance that allows you not only to endure the next decades of dentistry—but to enjoy it.

If you're an owner like me, then I hope that this was useful for you. I hope that you can examine your office systems and culture to see what's working and what isn't. I've offered many essential strategies that can help you improve communication and efficiency. Remember, you can take good care of your people and your patients without doing harm to yourself.

I wrote this book with everyone in mind, including the people who are struggling so much that they feel like they're drowning. For you, I want you to know there's hope and there's help. Yes, you *can* make your work experience better.

There are a lot of people out there who have the experience you need and who want to help you—therapists, coaches, consultants, and fellow dentists. Reach out—they can help you put your insides in order so you can, in turn, put your office in order.

> *Burnout isn't going to get the best of you. I've been there, and by using these strategies, now I am stronger, happier, and I look forward to going to work every day. But, it didn't happen overnight and took a lot of hard work. I'm proof you can go through burnout and come out on the other side happy to go to work every day. I know you can do it too.*
>
> –DR. ERIC BLOCK

Email me at info@thestressfreedentist.com if you have any questions regarding any of my stories, tips, or systems. You can also join a group of like-minded dentists to get peer support on my Facebook, Instagram, and LinkedIn pages: @thestressfreedentist and, since we're all very busy people, here are the summaries of the preceding chapters.

What is Burnout?

- Burnout isn't stress. Burnout is what you get when you've had unaddressed stress for too long.
- Burnout is a real thing with real symptoms.
- Burnout is very common among dentists.
- Burnout gets worse when it's ignored.
- There's hope! Take action now.

Depression, Anxiety, Addiction, and Pain

- The apathy of depression is actually a protective mechanism. Your brain is numbing you out because you're in pain. If you can address the stress, then you can hopefully help your brain feel safe enough that it will let you feel things again.
- Anxiety is uncomfortable, but it's common and treatable. If you're feeling the symptoms listed here, reach out and get help.
- Addiction is fed by shame. If your life is changing and you're withdrawing, take a look at your coping mechanisms and know that you can get help and that you're not alone.
- All pain is pain. Emotional pain and physical pain—it's all brain-pain. Do whatever you can to address the sources of your pain. Don't try to ignore it; it'll just get worse. It won't go away on its own, but it can be treated.
- Fix your work-life balance by finding ways to leave dentistry at the office mentally and physically. You can't look forward to going to work if you never leave it in the first place.
- Find your yoga, whether it's actually yoga or not. Do what you need to do to decompress from the day-to-day grind of dentistry.
- Make your office a welcoming place to be that is geared towards preserving your mental and physical health.
- Finally, if you're having thoughts of despair or self-harm, please talk to someone. Call the National Suicide Prevention Lifeline, a 24-hour service. 800-273-8255

People-Pleasing and Conflict Resolution

- People-pleasing is a natural reaction to anxiety and being in a new situation.
- Associates may not control the office but can still set boundaries in their everyday work lives.
- Assess and address any issues you have with rejection and abandonment to decrease your anxiety.
- Transform your conflict avoidance into confidence by learning conflict resolution—then you won't be as afraid to speak up and say "NO."
- Don't set yourself on fire to keep someone else warm.

Imposter Syndrome

- Imposter syndrome can affect anyone, but especially those with perfectionism, anxiety, or depression, minorities or anyone underrepresented in their field, or those who've recently had a major life change.
- There are several subtypes of imposter syndrome; you may be one, two, or all of them.
- Imposter syndrome is exhausting and contributes to burnout.
- Get help from a therapist, mentor, or coach to address your fears that lead to imposter syndrome and reset your expectations from impossibly high to reasonable and attainable.
- Reach out for support from peers whom you trust and be yourself.

How to Handle Rejection and Connect With Patients

- It's normal to fear rejection. Figure out the root of your fear and take it seriously.
- Case selection is your friend. Learn how to spot red flag patients, and refer out patients who are not a good fit.
- Find whatever help you need with learning communication skills. Read books, connect with peers, find mentors, work with a coach.
- Don't care more about someone's mouth (or job!) than they do.
- Bad reviews are a fact of life. Build a process, trust it's there, and let go of the fear.

Office Culture—Is Yours Toxic?

- Toxic work cultures increase the anxiety that leads to people-pleasing and accelerates burnout.
- Toxic work culture is marked by a lack of honesty, communication, and accountability.
- You can either keep toxic culture or keep good employees, but not both.
- Owners and leaders must act to increase accountability and communication.
- Associates may not control the office but can still set boundaries in their everyday work lives.

Don't Let Money Burn You

- Know your numbers. If numbers worry you, hire someone trustworthy to help you understand and work them.
- Expecting perfection means planning to be stressed out. Persistent is better than perfect.
- Use benchmarks to bridge the gap between budget forecasts and business reality.
- If you're thinking about transitioning to owner, evaluate the prospective practice's financial state and your own emotional and physical state.
- Quick daily audits can help prevent embezzlement.

Business Management and Boundaries

- Don't pick favorites. Doing so will negatively impact your work environment.
- Don't gossip about employees—ever. You are the boss; act like one.
- Make sure all policies are in writing.
- Make sure your written policies include proper use of the practice's computers and phones.
- Have disciplinary steps in an employee handbook, no matter how small your practice is.
- Deal with inappropriate behavior immediately, and make sure you're providing a safe work environment.
- Have an open-door policy for your employees to be able to come and share concerns.

- Have a grievance box that employees can put notes in. Have this box in a discreet place, like a break room or bathroom.
- Do something! Your team needs strong leadership. If you aren't able to provide it, then find a business coach who can help you to develop that skill.

Resources

Block Burnout with Solid Systems and Automations

Here are some resources I didn't have room for in the preceding chapters. We, dentists, are not only learning business management on the go but also fine-tuning our clinical procedures. I've found it helpful to have detailed step-by-step workflows for not only my own clinical procedure but for the office manager and staff as well. Such as making temporary crowns, policy on x-rays, cleaning and prepping rooms, how to conduct one-on-one employee reviews, and how to respond to a bad review. Knowing I have a step-by-step plan for handling each aspect of running a practice helps me feel less anxious and more in control.

How to Respond to a Bad Review

I used to replay certain procedures or patient interactions over and over in my head, whether I was at work or home; this fear was what disrupted my work/life balance. I would think about all the "what ifs" and envision worst-case scenarios.

Anxiety sounds like a constant "what if" or "I'm sure this will be terrible" in your head. One way to manage that anxiety is to answer that *if* with a *then*.

Therapy, prescribed anti-anxiety medications, and getting comfortable with who I am were useful ways for me to address my anxiety personally, and step-by-step procedures like these have been useful for me in addressing that anxiety professionally.

First, some things to remember about bad reviews:

They're going to happen. Even though my mom says everyone likes me, that isn't reality. You can't avoid bad reviews in your entire career—they will happen. Don't get personally offended when they happen. You can't please 100 percent of the people 100 percent of the time.

Offer a way to give direct feedback. Sometimes patients just need an outlet to complain. If you have a way for them to give you feedback directly, where they can feel heard, you may be able to avoid a bad social media review where everyone can see.

It's probably not about you. If you're constantly getting bad reviews about the same issues, then figure out the problem and fix it, but in my experience, many bad reviews aren't even related to the dentist or the procedures. They are more often due to staff, insurance, or financial miscommunications.

Some bad reviews are actually good. It would look suspicious if you had all five-star reviews. Having a few bad reviews in the mix adds social credibility. I discuss this in a podcast interview with Dr. Len Tau in episode number fourteen of my Deals for Dentists podcast. Check it out!

Your best defense is a great offense. It's impossible to prevent bad reviews. The best tactic is to bury the bad reviews with good reviews. Reviews are the backbone of your marketing, and so long as you maintain a favorable ratio of compliments to complaints, you're going to be okay.

With that in mind, here's my process for answering a bad review online:

1. *Respond.* Drop the "We don't typically respond" non-response. It's better to respond and take action.
2. In your written response, consider inviting them to call you to discuss the matter. The key phrase I use here is, "Your health is always of prime importance to us."
3. *Keep things general.* Speak generically and not specifically; speak professionally and not personally. Don't get into the nitty-gritty. Keep your response's focus on your policies. For instance, if a patient's review objects to your x-ray policy, then speak generally to that by reinforcing in your response that x-rays are a standard industry-accepted practice to ensure the patient's good health.
4. *Keep things positive.* I would acknowledge the review's concerns by saying something about how you're very sorry to hear that the patient felt the way they did. Then I would add that how they felt was never your intention and that your office's primary concerns are both their health and ensuring a great experience in your office.
5. *Maintain the moral high ground.* Even if the reviewer resorts to name-calling, make sure you come back as over-the-top nice and accommodating. This is a great way to run a business anyway, but it's also a great way to maintain that high ground for those witnessing the exchange online. Even if you can't convince the reviewer, your positive and professional response will convince others reading your reviews that you're not the asshole in this situation.
6. *Keep a script.* In my office, we give our people a form to use whenever a negative review pops up.

Sample script

Thank you so much for your honest feedback. We really appreciate you taking the time to leave a review and bring this to our attention.

We're sorry your experience with us was not a positive one, and we want to do everything in our power to make it right.

If you have any additional feedback, would you consider giving us a call? We would love to hear from you!

Sincerely, [Practice's Name/Doctor's Name]

This helps anyone else viewing your negative review see that you are proactive in wanting to help and solve a problem a patient had. Whether the review is legitimate or not, responding positively, professionally, and publicly can help keep your practice's reputation intact online and can put your worries to rest.

How to Conduct Executive Staff Check-ins (ESCs)

How do we keep employees happy and work less stressful? One-on-ones.

ESC sessions are a great way to connect with each staff member. These can be performed by the dentist or an office manager, depending on your preference. One-on-ones are a great way to keep a good pulse on the culture of what's really going on in your office. Some staffers may be hesitant to open up, so it's important to let them know that they are not in trouble! Reassure them that you or your office manager is just checking in on them to see how leaders can help support them and that the interview will be confidential.

Because the goal of ESCs are to find out how your team member is doing in their work-life, it's important for them to do most of the talking. I try to help them open up by prompting them with some feedback on how they're doing—what they're doing well and what they could use improvement on. I also try to ask questions to see if they have concerns or issues. The main thing is to help keep the conversation flowing so that they'll share openly with you. It's like a mini life-coaching session.

I recommend doing these quarterly for your regular staff, but a bit more often for new hires. This will be so much more productive than just doing a once-a-year annual review. Document these conversations, and read your notes to prepare for the next meeting.

Your staff will appreciate it and create a happier, safer, and less stressful environment for everyone. They will also work harder knowing that they are being held accountable, as you will be having this type of meeting with them again in a few months to review the job performance goals that you'd discussed and agreed upon.

If you want to know more about the benefits of one-on-one interviews and how to best conduct them, I recommend Paul Etchison's book *Dental Practice Hero*.

Stress-Free Procedure Workflows

I just finished a composite filling—it was great. My assistants and I have it down to a step-by-step routine with no wasted time. I hate waiting for things, so I constantly need to be doing something productive. I remember a new hire assistant said to me on one of her first days, "I can't read your mind." I said, "You will soon!" We both laughed, but after doing these procedures over and over and with the same workflows, they become automatic for your staff. Eventually, they will be one step ahead of you and make your procedures so much more stress-free.

Here is a typical scenario that I have the staff trained to do. Everyone knows their role, and it makes my life easier.

Typical Restorative Procedure Workflow:

The patient is escorted to the operatory. The assistant will confirm the date of birth, review their medical history, confirm the planned procedure and teeth to be worked on, and ask if there are any questions. If the patient is nervous, they know to offer a squeezy or two, sunglasses, headphones for music, chapstick, or a blanket and pillow. We also offer nitrous oxide for phobic patients.

The assistant will recline the patient, give them protective eyewear, and place the topical benzocaine where the site of the injection is going.

They will message me that the patient is ready and topical is in. We use an internal messaging service called Weave, but there are many others that can help you quickly message between rooms and workstations.

I respond to the message, "I'll be right in!" and head to the operatory. Once there, I make some chit-chat and take the topical out, review the planned procedure and teeth to be worked on, and ask if there are any questions. If not, I then get them numb.

After a little more chit-chat, I tell them, "Let's let this Novocain soak in for a few minutes, and I'll be right back to check on you. I make my way to my back office to my comfy office chair or Yogibo.

I have a joke for the new staff. As I leave the room, I will say "Bii!" which sounds like a goat saying Byeeeeee. "B.I.I." stands for Burs (get my burs ready), Ice (ice test the tooth after a few minutes to make sure it's numb), Isolation (insert the Isolite or vacuLUX isolation device). If we are doing a crown, the assistant also knows to book their next appointment, get a shade and a preliminary impression to use for the temporary crown, and start scanning with our intraoral scanner. They will message me when all of this is done, and they are ready for me to come back into the room.

The staff will message me the results of the ice test. Game Changer Alert: it's very important to ice test the teeth to confirm the patient is numb before moving to the next step. I never take a bur to a tooth unless they pass the endo ice test! There is nothing more stressful than a patient that is not fully numb and who feels pain during a procedure. The ice test is also a great way to help a patient calm down because it relieves the fear that they will feel pain during the procedure.

If the patient passed the ice test, then they know to insert the isolation device, and then it's drill time. If they still felt some discomfort with the endo ice, then I get them more numb. No icey, then no drilley. My burs are all laid out for me. I go step-by-step with each bur—each one has a purpose, and there are some extras of each close by. I throw out dull burs and replace them. I also have extra handpieces in case the one I'm using stalls on me.

Again, there is no wasted time. Each room is well-stocked in case I need something replaced mid-procedure. We also try to keep each room stocked the same, so staff knows where everything is. There is nothing more frustrating than when the staff is opening and closing drawers looking for something, or worse, they can't find it and have to leave the room to go get it.

For crowns and fillings, I go from bur to bur in a chronological sequence, and I do it the same way every time. This consistency is key because it makes this part of the procedure automatic for both me and my assistant.

My assistants are well-trained to remove any cord and make a chairside provisional. I have shown them and had them practice multiple times on a typodont until they prove they are ready to do it on a live patient. Like I mentioned earlier, my assistants have repeated these procedures so many times with me that the repetitions become second nature. I barely even have to talk to my assistants anymore because we've trained in this procedure pas de deux so many times.

***Game Changer Alert: Pre-op and mid-procedure intra-oral camera photos for any restorative procedure, especially if it involves caries I will always take a photo of the decay to show the patient.

For interproximal restorations, once the isolation device is in and the patient is confirmed numb, I start with a SS White GW-1 bur to start my box prep, so I can excavate decay. Sometimes I use a caries indicator and an appropriately-sized slow-speed carbide round bur to finish removing all of the decay. When I do this, I warn the patient that things may get a little bumpy. Caries removal is something that took me time to perfect. A lot of it is by feel with the slow speed round bur and with the help of caries indicator.

Crowns

I based my technique off of Dr. Mike Ditolla's reverse crown preparation technique. I have altered it to my own style; the key is consistency. My crown procedure is the same thing every time.

I start with a round diamond and make my marginal prep, then break contact with a 330 carbide, and also make my occlusal reduction depth cuts with the 330 since it is about 1.5mm of cutting length. I then finish the occlusal clearance with a diamond football bur and finish my prep with the diamond of choice, depending on the material I have the lab use.

I tell the assistant which cord size I want and if I just need it for a specific area or if I need it all around the tooth. Sometimes I pack double cord to get a good retraction or Ferric sulfate for hemostasis. After retraction, I scan and adjust the prep or reduction if needed. Then my job is done, and the assistant makes the temporary. Patients (especially the gaggers) absolutely love the intra-oral scanner. We have the Trios 3 shape, and they are so impressed with the technology and do not have to deal with the goopy impressions. #Return-on-fun

I make sure I have broken the gingival floor contact so I can easily get the matrix band in. For Class 2 restorations, I use the V-3 system from Ultradent and the Automatrix from Garrison. I always make sure to break the contact with a flame bur, then place the appropriate size band, the wedge, and the sectional matrix. If I am doing back-to-back Class 2 composites (MO and DO), then I will fill the first restoration using an Automatrix and good fitting wedge. It's important to make sure to have a good seal with no bleeding. I didn't always do this, but the bleeding messes everything up. I always make sure that I can't see the wedge from inside the box. If you can't see the wedge, then you know the band is sealed tightly around the margins of your prep. If you can see the wedge, then it is not sealed, and you may get moisture, overhangs, or flossing issues.

If everything looks good, then I burnish the matrix band down by the gingival/middle third of the adjacent tooth. I don't want the band burnished too tight by the occlusal 3rd; this could make for difficulty with flossing.

Then I start with a microprime to clean out the prep and prevent sensitivity and bond of choice. I currently use Prime and Bond Elect One Step Bond and cure with the Valo light. I cover all the exposed dentin and the walls of the prep with Flow-It, and then finish the restoration with GC Universal Flo. For anterior teeth, I use Omnichroma's One Shade Composite.

I cure it, take the matrix band out, and then re-cure it. I make adjustments with my round carbide bur until I am pretty sure the occlusion looks right.

The isolation device is removed, and the assistant immediately has the patient bite on the articulating paper.

We direct the patient to bite and grind "hard" on the articulating paper. I make sure to emphasize the "hard on your back teeth" to make sure they are giving it a really good grind. Otherwise, it is hard for them to perceive if they are fully biting due to the anesthesia. Also, make sure their lips and tongue are out of the way for this step; nobody wants a patient to bite and injure their numb tongue or cheek so that they end up calling back in when their local wears off.

Also, pre-operatively it's a good habit to check their bite before they are numb just to make sure there isn't anything out of the ordinary like a class three edge to edge bite or a unique crossbite or mal-occlusion. But telling them to bite and grind hard will ensure good marks on the tooth so you can adjust the filling.

I spend a lot of time making sure the occlusion is ideal and that there are no blue marks left on the filling material. My goal isn't to make it look like amazing composite restorations with tertiary anatomy that we were taught in dental school or that you see in some ads or journal articles. I want the marks to be on natural tooth structure because once the local wears off, I don't want the patient to feel like their occlusion is off and that they're contacting that filling first. They will call and come back in or, worse, develop pain. Like the proximal contacts, if I get it right while the patient is in the chair, then everyone is happy.

Game Changer Alert: I also don't ask, "How's your bite feel?" At this point, the patient is numb and usually has a poor perception of an accurate bite. Asking them to think about their bite when they don't have sensory feedback is a waste of time. I recommend you skip this back and forth. The occlusal marks are far more accurate—use them to guide this part of the process. Some patients (you know the ones I'm talking about) will neurotically overthink their occlusion and will sit there for five minutes testing their bite.

I finish the occlusion and check the floss and polish. Make sure the floss gets a good snap! If not, then best to re-do the filling right then and there. It will only take a few minutes, and if you don't, then the patient may call back due to food impaction, and then you will have to go through the entire process of anesthetizing and prepping all over again. That's a major waste of everyone's time and energy. Check the snap of the floss to make sure you get it right the first time.

I always get a good proximal contact with the ball burnishing with the v3 matrix. I used to struggle with open proximal contacts, and patients would come back annoyed by food impaction, but this dials it in.

Sticking with the no wasted time philosophy, during the few moments the assistant is removing any matrix materials or checking the occlusion, I start readying the intraoral images to show the patient or will start writing notes in my templates. Templates are a huge timesaver and create less stress. I used to worry about my notes and if they were board-level notes in case I got sued or taken to the board, but now my notes are all templates and are well crafted.

Then, the procedure is done!

I have the patient take their protective sunglasses off and show them the photos of the decay. Game Changer Alert: this shows them proof, and they own the issue. There is no issue with patients saying a filling should have never been done when you show them this photo. A documented photo is worth a thousand words, and having that easy-to-see proof for a patient will dispel a lot of anxiety in a dentist.

I also tell them, due to the amount of decay seen here, there is a chance you may need a crown or endo. They see the photo, and I document all of this. They usually say something like, "Wow, that's gross! Thanks so much."

This system of going step by step makes so much less stress for me, my staff, and our patients. It's automatic, and a lot of patients will say, "That was fast!" or "That wasn't so bad!" or "Wow, you two were a well-oiled machine." Everyone leaves satisfied, and most of the time, the patient is not calling back with complaints of food impaction or their bite feeling off.

Anaesthesia technique

This is such a crucial part of being a dentist and creating that ultimate patient experience. Like one of my favorite Pink Floyd songs, you must keep your patients comfortably numb. And remember to always use the ice test prior to picking up the handpiece.

Here are my techniques:

Upper teeth and lower anteriors and premolars

I will just do buccal infiltration with one or two carpules of septocaine, depending on how many teeth were working on. If still not numb, then I'll give a pdl injection (not with a ligajet but just with my regular syringe). I give as much pressure as I can until the tissue blanches. I typically administer about a one-fourth carpule. Sometimes (but very rarely), I will have to give a palatal injection when doing restorative.

For any surgery like implants or extractions, I give the palatal injection every time. Patients hate this one, so I'll press a q-tip with topical on the palatal site and tell them right before that, "this one is gonna wake you up in the morning."

In any situation when administering the first dose of local anesthetic, if they are feeling the injection and motioning that they are in a lot of pain then I will just give a little bit to get the area numb, wait a few minutes and then give the follow up injections which will be much easier for them. If you don't stop and give the patient a break, and the patient starts holding their breath, then not only does it make for a poor experience, but it increases any chances of syncope.

Lower molars (the grand-daddy of them all!)

I start with a mandibular block of lidocaine, and I tell the patient, "I'm going to check back in a few minutes, and what we are looking for is the corner of your lip and chin to start to feel numb. Your tongue on that side will probably get numb first, but the key is the lip and chin. It usually takes more than one dose." So they are expecting it and not surprised or frustrated or nervous when I give them more than one dose.

I come back in and check. If there's still no lip or chin action, then I will give another mandibular block carpule, but this time a little higher than the first one just in case their nerve branch anatomy is unique. Sometimes, if the patient is super relaxed and easy to work on, then I will just give two mandibular blocks back to back, one a little higher than the other.

Once the lip and chin are feeling fuzzy, then I'll give a pdl injection on the buccal and lingual and a long buccal.

Wait another five minutes and ice test. Make sure you've explained the difference between cold sensation/pain versus pressure. Sometimes patients who don't understand this difference will interpret the ice test's pressure as pain, and they're actually numb. You don't want to waste time giving more injections.

If they still feel the ice test, then I will move on to the Tuttle Numb Now (TNN) technique which was developed by Dr. Gregory Tuttle: *https://tuttlenumbnow.com/*

This will do the trick 99.9 percent of the time, and the patients get totally numb, and I can get to work without those stressful, tense moments, wondering if the patient is going to feel any pain at any point during the procedure.

Temporary Crown Workflow

I train my assistants to make a "five-minute temp." I have them practice on the typodont and show them my technique. My assistants used to spend twenty to thirty minutes fabricating and seating their temporary crowns, and it is just too long for them and the patients.

The more efficient they can make the provisional, the less chance the patient's local will wear off, and the quicker the assistant can finish and get ready for the next room. Taking too long with a temp crown is not a good look, and it sets everyone back in the schedule.

For anterior esthetic cases, however, I will have a lab-made temporary fabricated and ready to go.

For your typical cases, here are my tips for a five-minute temp:

Pre-operatively and while the patient is getting numb = take a preliminary impression

- Teeth with fractured cusp,
    - You can add some cavit or wax or composite to the broken area before taking the preliminary impression or
    - You can remove some material where the tooth was broken after the impression was taken.

- Inspect the preliminary impression to make sure you got all of the pre-prepped tooth.
- When it's time to make the temporary crown be sure to squeeze a little temp material out before putting on the mixing tip to ensure both base and catalyst materials are flowing. Sometimes if the material was left out or hadn't been used in a while, one of the materials will flow more than the other and affect the setting.
- Place the tip and put material into the prepped tooth in the preliminary impression and insert it into the mouth. I also recommend placing a little on the table to test for when it starts to set up and harden
- Take out of mouth after the material starts to harden up slightly. I use bisacryl, and it is usually a minute and fifteen seconds.
- Don't wait too long and let it fully harden in the mouth and have a chance to get into undercuts which will make it difficult to remove without breaking it.
- Once the impression has been removed from the mouth, it may be on the tooth or still inside the impression. Leave out to fully harden a couple of minutes
- Clean off any excess material in the mouth while this is happening

Trimming the Temp

- Pencil to mark mesial and distal contact areas
- Turn upside down and trim under contact areas and around the temp to make smooth/rounded
- Trim above the contact area and buccal and lingual of it just leaving a little pencil mark left

- Smooth down occlusion—flatten out temp aggressively
- Hold the temp right side up and look down on it. Adjust any square areas that need to be rounded off
- Try it in the mouth.
- If it won't seat, then trim mesial and distal proximal contact areas. Make sure no excess material is stuck on the tooth
- Try occlusal paper. Trim it, so it has a small blue contact point. Like with my composite filling technique, I will have the patient bite and grind hard on the paper to ensure a proper mark. I don't even ask them how their bite feels because they are numb, and typically, they don't have an accurate perception of their bite.
- Polish
- Cement
- Clean up cement
- Give take-home instructions and package of extra temp cement

Crown insert appointment

This used to be a stressful procedure for me, but now with our digital scanner and our automatic appointment flow, it is one of the least stressful parts of my day. I know that I had enough occlusal reduction and proper margins during my prep because I evaluated them with my intraoral scanner before sending the case to the lab. Like I mentioned earlier, we use the 3Shape Trios Intra Oral Scanner and have been very happy with it. We also spend a little extra and use a good reliable lab, and it is worth every penny. I used to try and save some money by sending my cases to a cheap lab, and the frustration of all the crown adjustments was not worth the savings.

My assistant typically takes off the temp, cleans up the cement, tries on the crown, and takes an x-ray. Sometimes the crown does not seat, and they just leave it for me to try it in. Either way, the assistant alerts me when they're ready for me to come in.

I always make sure I have the flossing contacts perfect first. I don't bother checking the margins or bite until I know the proximal contacts are not too tight and that the crown is seated all the way.

Then, after adjusting the proximal, I'll have the patient bite and grind hard on the blue carbon paper. The bite may force the crown to seat a bit more, creating a tighter proximal contact. I check with floss again to make sure it's not too tight. I do this over and over until I have confirmed the perfect flossing contacts. I then check the margins and adjust the occlusion as needed.

Before cementation, I will tell the patient, "This may feel very cold, but will get better," and warn them of possible cementation sensitivity.

I then have my assistant mix the cement, and I fill it up and push the crown on the tooth with my fingers, and then rock my fingers around, pushing down. Sometimes you think the crown is down all the way, but if you rock it and push in a certain direction, it may seat more. I can pretty much tell that it's in when I see excess cement extrude out of all directions.

I quickly clean up some of the cement with a cotton roll or brush and then have them bite down hard on a cotton roll. I tell the patient, "Give it firm pressure for about fifteen seconds." At this point, you will typically see a little more cement seep out; that's how I know it's fully seated. Clean the cement up quickly before it hardens. If you act fast, then you'll be able to peel it off with a scaler.

Then I will then make sure I can get the floss through and have the patient bite down for another minute.

Crown insert appointments are one of the few times I will actually ask the patient how their bite feels. They typically aren't numb and have a good sense if something isn't quite right.

If they say it feels good, I will ask them, "Are you sure?" because now is the time to get it right.

Just like with my composite fillings, what I don't do is send the patient home with a light proximal contact. The patient will nearly always get food impacted in it and will call you and need to come back in, where you may have to redo the case. Nobody likes this outcome.

Shade Taking

For shade-taking, we use the Vita Linearguide 3D-Master shade guide. I use this shade guide because it's made my life easier and less stressful. It has a great system for picking the perfect shade and makes my life easier and less stressful, which is definitely worth the money.

We also like to take the shade early in the appointment while the teeth are nice and hydrated. For anterior high aesthetic cases, I will have the patient very involved in the shade selection process. We will pick a shade together in front of a mirror near the window, which has natural light. Getting a good shade is crucial.

For posterior teeth, getting the wrong shade is a waste of everyone's time. For anterior teeth, it is more challenging and usually involves a lot of photographs and patient and lab communication.

When matching shade, tempering patient expectations is key! For example, I may say, "Mr. Jones, we may get lucky and get this on the first try—but usually, it takes two or three tries to get it right." I'll repeat this expectation in conversation a few more times to ensure that no one is too frustrated if the shade doesn't initially match, and the case needs to be sent back to the lab.

However, if you have a great local lab, then you can always send the patient for a custom shade if they offer that service.

Stress-Free Morning Checklist

Assistant Checklist

- Check oxygen and ER kit.
- Turn on main switches, computers, and x-ray units.
- Confirm rooms are clean. Check floors (sometimes there will be a wedge, cotton roll, or string of floss that was overlooked. Sit in chairs for patients' perspectives—fix what's missed.
- Confirm all lab cases are back for today and tomorrow.
- Confirm rooms are well stocked with supplies. Every room should be a mini stock room of 90 percent of commonly used things such as burs, handpieces, basics kits, and composite/crown set up in each room.
- Check the intraoral cameras are on and working.
- Charge curing light batteries.
- Set up rooms for the first and second patients.
- Make sure the chair is in a ready position, and the chair power is on.

Throughout the Day

- Keep inventory control throughout the day. Constantly check the supply of materials and write down any needed supplies, including any necessary information about how much of which items.

- Catch up on *cleaning the treatment rooms*, tubs, and trays, stocking treatment rooms and burs, organizing stock closets, and more.
- Treatment rooms should look immaculate at all times. This cannot be emphasized enough.
- Keep an eye on the schedule, and help others as needed.

End of the Day

- Ensure all operatories are clean, set up for the next day's first patients, and chairs are raised to their highest point
- Lights are off
- Purge lines for high-speeds and A/W syringes
- Remove all instruments from the Biosonic
- Ensure all instruments are bagged and ready to go for the sterilization cycle
- Clean lab, including countertop and sink, and turn off all equipment
- Ensure all models are poured, trimmed, and labeled
- Prepare all lab cases
- Turn off the autoclave
- Tomorrow's routing slips ready
- Tomorrow's lab cases ready
- Prepare for tomorrow's morning huddle
- Shut off items in the lab: lights, sandblaster, lab motor

Stress-Free Hygiene Checklist

Every Morning

Make sure the camera and x-rays are working each morning before the first patient
  Check if any NP's x-rays are confirmed here or missing

- Confirm patient's DOB and medical history
- Profile picture if needed
- Mark if there will be an exam, and which doctor is to do the exam
- Does the patient have any issues or complaints?
- Take necessary x-rays/photos. Don't forget anterior PA's if needed. Use clinical judgment
- Take photos of recession and restorations, and show patients any potential issues, especially large amalgams or any fracture lines.
- Any interproximal areas on x-rays or suspicious areas to warn the doctor about?
- Take PA if needed for crowns etc.
- Any red previously tx planned areas to hone in on and re-discuss
- Any perio issues/probings?
- Any clenching or grinding, need a night guard? More people are clenching/grinding their teeth than ever due to stress
- Is the patient interested in fluoride varnish or bleaching?
- Weave—data gathering is completed, then weave-message me of any issues or patient concerns
- Start prophylactics
- I want them to message me after data gathering and before the prophy begins to give me enough time to review and come in

early in the appointment. This way, I avoid the hygienist from running late or having to wait for me to come in for the exam.
- Document why restorations are needed and on which surfaces. Example: decay on mesial, food impaction, fractured porcelain, stick with explorer, visible decay, pain, etc.
- Schedule recall and if any other visits are needed. Be clear on what n.v. will be done.
- Use visual aids to show what a crown is.
- Ask if family member needs a cleaning

Stress-Free Culture and Mission Statement

At Acton Dental, we have a "team-oriented" environment. We are all working together for the good of the patients and the success of the practice.

If someone is out, then everyone should be pulling together to help. There is no "that's not my job" kind of attitude in this office. If one person needs help, we help them.

Communicate with patients in an understandable and professional way.

No whispering around patients.

Stress-Free Appointment Scheduling

- New patient adults 90 min
- New patient children 50-60 min
- Adult pro 60 min
- Adult pro with fmx or extra time needed 60 min
- Child pro 40 min

- 1 hour for 2 quadrants of sc/rp
- Do not violate Sc/rp blocks or new patient slots unless within 48 hours.
- Limited scale 1-3 teeth 30min
- Full mouth debridement 60 min (no exam allowed)
- Sealants 30 min

General guideline for doctor's time schedule (subject to change case by case and clinician to clinician)

- Implant surgery 90 min
- Crown 80-90 min
- 1 filling 30 min
- 2 or more fillings 40-60 min
- Scan for night guard, bleaching trays, temporaries, rpd/dentures 30 min.
- Try in or delivery of these removable procedures 30 min
- Nitrous patients may need to add 10 more minutes
- Consult 30 min (if implant consult = include ct scan in appointment)
- Post-op some can be side booked
- Careful not to side book in the middle of a procedure. Ideally, side book a patient at the beginning of another procedure while the other patient is getting numb.
- Ideally, no side booking during a nitrous patient or surgery patient.

Stress-Free office scheduling protocols: The Schedule Begins at 8:00 a.m.

The schedule is the most important thing in an efficient, low-stress practice.

Everyone needs to keep an eye on the entire schedule. Also, make sure someone "owns" it, whether the doctors or the hygienists schedule to fill holes.

Establish succession: if the schedule owner isn't at the practice, who is next in line to take on that ownership and do that job?

Make rules like "do not violate the np/sc/rp/crown/er slots." The goal is to keep the perfect day schedule.

Create the "perfect day schedule" ideal, and create rules that lead to that ideal. Prime spots are 8:00 a.m. and after 3:00 p.m. Schedule from the middle of the day out.

Know your patients and their needs and potential areas of flexibility.

For instance, patients that commute to work and who may get stuck in traffic are best scheduled before 8:00 a.m. or on a Saturday. Retired patients can be seen in the middle of the day instead of a high-demand slot.

Take care when scheduling teenagers and college kids in the morning because they're likely to sleep in. Keep slots open for kids during vacation weeks, and a shortlist of students home for the quick call list.

Make sure you have a central place for non-clinical notes about patients that both hygiene and the front desk can quickly reference. These notes will include things like "patient is back for school vacation during this time" or "patient can only come in on Thursdays."

Stress-free phone training and frequently asked questions

Phone training is very important. The phone is considered the most important piece of equipment in a dental office.

It is the patient or potential patient's first point of contact with the office.

We answer the phone with a clear, pleasant voice "Acton Dental Associates. This is _____. How may I help you?"

Practice and training should be ongoing. If you need help, ask for help on how to answer such common questions like:

Does my insurance cover this?

Price shoppers asking how much a procedure costs?

What to say when people try to cancel. "Don't say she's just calling to cancel."

How to discuss tx plans and financials.

How to answer insurance, care credit, and membership plan questions, etc.

Acton Dental Associates follows the American Dental Association Exam and Radiograph Recommendations

Acton Dental's Stress-Free Exam policy

Exams are performed twice a year by a dentist. Typically six months apart, especially high-risk patients (history of fillings, crowns, periodontal issues, etc.).

Patients must be examined by a dentist at least once a year

Note: Some patients may refuse a six-month exam but can't go more than a year.

New patients must have a comprehensive exam. Depending on their benefits, this may not be a covered benefit due to frequency.

Have Clear Financial Policies & Collections

Copays are due at the time of service

For lab cases (lab-made temporaries, crowns, dentures, partials, implants, etc.), the patient pays 50 percent upfront.

What credit cards are accepted? Visa and Mastercard. Not Amex or Discover.

Bounced check policy

Sending patients to collections policy?

Waiving small co-pays are case by case

Financial options

Determining the Options

Payment is at the time of service. If need be, payment can be split over appointments if the treatment takes more than one visit. Such as at crown impression and crown insert.

While making financial arrangements, present the patient with a written treatment estimate; have the patient sign one copy and keep one copy in the patient's record, even if the office is chartless. A lot of practice management software now has patient portal capabilities.

Patients with Dental Benefits "Insurance"

Dental insurance should ideally be referred to as Dental Benefits. It is not actually insurance but is a benefit from their employer. It is the plan their employer or they chose. We may be in or out of the network, depending on the plan. We must educate that insurance companies like to deny, delay, decline and are not looking out for the best interest of the patient. We are currently in-network for _____. We have signed a contract with these companies and have contracted fees with them.

We are out of network for _____.

1. Tell the patient how much the insurance company is expected to pay.
2. Tell the patient you will bill the insurance company for that amount.
3. Inform the patient they are responsible for that amount if the insurance company doesn't pay.
4. Collect the balance at the time of service (may charge with the credit card on file).

What is our policy if insurance hasn't paid after thirty, forty-five, sixty, ninety days?

What is our policy if the patient hasn't paid their copay?

Pretreatment estimates or Pre-determinations

We want to minimize the amount of PTE's (typically only offered for treatment of large cases that may be complex).

PTE's offer no guarantee and just end up delaying treatment.

We want to be insurance savvy, not insurance driven

I only use insurance to my advantage, like at the end of the year, use it or lose it situation. Or the beginning of the year, "great, you have new benefits for this year."

Implants can be placed and restored over two calendar years

What do you do when a patient is late, or you are late

The nature of dental care may require a longer than normal workday.

Late patients will be handled on a case by case basis.

Must document the tardiness and conversation.

We do as much as possible in the time left. If they made an effort to come in, even late, we should try not to turn them away.

Doctor's schedules are easier to accommodate patients that are late.

Hygiene late patients are more of a challenge due to schedule and chair availability.

Hi Mr. _____, I will do as much as time will permit in your allowed time slot. As it stands, we have time to do _____ and _____ but _____ is most likely not going to be completed today. Do you want to reschedule or do as much as possible today?

If we have time to see the patient, why not do it, as long as it was made clear to the patient (in a respectful way) that we would do what we can in the time remaining.

Life happens. Be empathetic. Do what you can do in the remaining time without throwing off your schedule or keeping the next patient waiting.

Patients need to value the appointment. If you are educating them about what is taking place during their appointments and the importance of keeping them, great.

If they are habitually fifteen minutes late, tell them their appointment is at 10:45 a.m. when it is really at 11:00 a.m.

Repeat offenders should not be pre-appointed (case by case situation).

If there is a pattern and if someone cancels or no-shows more than twice, they go on a quick call list.

Good notes are essential (Patient commutes to and from Boston for work—maybe Saturday would be best).

For those patients, it's three strikes, and you're out. Either dismiss or shortlist them.

Or patients may need to pre-pay to hold their spot

Chronic lateness must not be tolerated.

REFERENCES

Are You Burned Out?

Butler, Jen. "How Real Dentists Conquer Real Stress." dentistryiq.com, December 5, 2018. https://www.dentistryiq.com/practice-management/practice-management-tips/article/16367701/how-real-dentists-conquer-real-stress.

Depression, Anxiety, Addiction, and Pain

Butler, Jen. "How Real Dentists Conquer Real Stress." dentistryiq.com, December 5, 2018. https://www.dentistryiq.com/practice-management/practice-management-tips/article/16367701/how-real-dentists-conquer-real-stress.

Lang, Randy. "Stress in Dentistry--It Could Kill You! ." orallhealthgroup.com, September 1, 2007. https://www.oralhealthgroup.com/features/stress-in-dentistry-it-could-kill-you/.

Eisenberger, Naomi I., Matthew D. Lieberman, and Kipling D. Williams. "Does Rejection Hurt? An FMRI Study of Social Exclusion." Science.sciencemag.org. American Association for the Advancement of Science, October 10, 2003. https://science.sciencemag.org/content/302/5643/290.full.

Kross, Ethan, Marc G. Berman, Walter Mischel, Edward E. Smith, and Tor D. Wager. "Social Rejection Shares Somatosensory Representations with Physical Pain." PNAS.org. National Academy of Sciences, April 12, 2011. https://www.pnas.org/content/108/15/6270.

Fogel, Alan. "Emotional and Physical Pain Activate Similar Brain Regions." Psychology Today. Sussex Publishers, April 19, 2012. https://www.psychologytoday.com/us/blog/body-sense/201204/emotional-and-physical-pain-activate-similar-brain-regions.

Simon, Gregory E. "Treating Depression in Patients with Chronic Disease: Recognition and Treatment Are Crucial; Depression Worsens the Course of a Chronic Illness." The Western Journal of Medicine. Copyright 2001 BMJ Publishing Group, November 2001. https://www.ncbi.nlm.nih.gov/pmc/articles/PMC1071593/.

Kelsch, Noel Brandon. "Risks of Dentistry to Personal Health." rdhmag.com, February 14, 2014. https://www.rdhmag.com/pathology/oral-pathology/article/16404240/risks-of-dentistry-to-personal-health.

Curtins, Eric K. "When Dentists Do Drugs: A Prescription for Prevention." dentistwellbeing.com, 2011. http://www.dentistwellbeing.com/pdf/DentistsDoDrugs.pdf.

Butler, Jen. "How Real Dentists Conquer Real Stress." dentistryiq.com, December 5, 2018. https://www.dentistryiq.com/practice-management/practice-management-tips/article/16367701/how-real-dentists-conquer-real-stress.

Burger, David. "ADA Wellness Survey Reveals Dentists' Ergonomic Issues." ada.org. American Dental Association, January 12, 2018. https://www.rdhmag.com/pathology/oral-pathology/article/16404240/risks-of-dentistry-to-personal-health.

People-Pleasing and Conflict Resolution

McKenzie, Sally. "Is One of These Common Problems Causing Stress in Your Dental Practice?" dentistryiq.com. Dentistry IQ, July 3, 2018. https://www.dentistryiq.com/practice-management/practice-management-tips/article/16367680/is-one-of-these-common-problems-causing-stress-in-your-dental-practice.

Imposter Syndrome

Butler, Jen. "How Real Dentists Conquer Real Stress." dentistryiq.com, December 5, 2018. https://www.dentistryiq.com/practice-management/practice-management-tips/article/16367701/how-real-dentists-conquer-real-stress.

Bravata, Dena M., Sharon A. Watts, Autumn L. Keefer, Divya K. Madhusudhan, Katie T. Taylor, Dani M. Clark, Ross S. Nelson, Kevin O. Cokley, and Heather K. Hagg. "Prevalence, Predictors, and Treatment of Impostor Syndrome: a Systematic Review." Journal of General Internal Medicine. U.S. National Library of Medicine, December 17, 2019. https://www.ncbi.nlm.nih.gov/pmc/articles/PMC7174434/.

Don't Let the Money Burn You

Stapley, K. "No One Is Totally Immune from Theft, Embezzlement." dentaleconomics.com. Dental Economics, 2011. www.dentaleconomics.com.

"An Agile Approach to Budgeting for Uncertain Times." Georgetown Chamber of Commerce & Industry, August 27, 2020. https://gcci.gy/an-agile-approach-to-budgeting-for-uncertain-times/.

Business Management with Boundaries

Greer, Andrea. "The Desperate Need for Business Education in Dentistry." dentistryiq.com. Dentistry IQ, June 20, 2018. https://www.dentistryiq.com/practice-management/practice-management-tips/article/16367683/the-desperate-need-for-business-education-in-dentistry.

How to Stay in Touch with Dr. Block

Go to *www.TheStressFreeDentist.com* to find out more information about online courses, podcasts, blogs, in-person events, and to join the Stress-Free Dentistry Facebook group to engage with like-minded dental professionals.

Go to *www.DealsforDentists.com* to find new customer offers from companies across the industry. Deals for Dentists brings the convention price directly to you.

Listen to the Deals for Dentists Podcast where Dr. Block interviews dental professionals and dental companies about how they are serving the industry.

You can also email Dr. Eric Block at *info@thestressfreedentist.com* with any questions or requests for speaking engagements.

Thanks for reading,

–Dr. Eric Block

THE STRESS-FREE DENTIST

Made in United States
North Haven, CT
17 February 2022